Market Guide for
YOUNG
WRITERS

Market Guide for
YOUNG
WRITERS

---

by Kathy Henderson

SHOE TREE PRESS
White Hall, Virginia

Published by
Shoe Tree Press, an imprint of Betterway Publications, Inc.
P.O. Box 219, Crozet, VA 22932
(804) 823-5661

Library of Congress Catalog Card Number: 87-62596

ISBN 0-936915-10-2

PRINTED IN THE UNITED STATES OF AMERICA
Second Printing/Second Edition

*To my husband, Keith, who
helped me become a published writer
while still young at heart*

Contents

Foreword

The first time I spoke with Kathy Henderson, two years ago, I felt an immediate kinship. I had called to acknowledge her new publication, the *Market Guide for Young Writers,* and to ask if she would list our children's magazine, *Shoe Tree,* in the next edition.

Our organization, the National Association for Young Writers, had been thinking about a similar project. We were aware that there were several publications that accepted children's writing, and had considered listing them in a pamphlet for our members. But, given our other projects and limited resources, we knew it would be a while before we would see this idea come to fruition. Imagine our excitement when we discovered such a book did, indeed, exist.

Since that time, Kathy Henderson has made invaluable contributions, in the form of time and energy, to the National Association for Young Writers. As an officer of the Board of Trustees, and our Executive Director, she works closely with children and teachers through workshops and conferences.

During that first conversation, I remember telling Kathy that I wished such a publication had existed when I was a child—a sentiment she herself shared and has since heard expressed many times. It is, in fact, the same reason I created our children's literary magazine. No such publication existed during those early years when, at the age of six, I took up my pencil and began to pour out story after story.

My audience—and yes, every writer, child or adult, must have one—was my family. The books I fashioned for them were crude—folded paper frequently held together by safety pins. The words and illustrations in these small books were my gifts to my family. Fortunately my family was a gracious group. They listened to every word, and most importantly, they gave me a gift in return, their encouragement. Especially my mother, who took one of the stories I had written when I was eight and typed it into legible form—my handwriting was atrocious even at that early stage—then passed it along to a friend of hers who was an elementary school teacher. The story was a melodramatic little tale about a troll and an elf. Over half the words were spelled phonetically, a common practice for me since I loved words and chose to use them even though they had not yet appeared on my second-grade spelling list. Fortunately my mother, unlike some of my teachers, overlooked the misspelled words. It was the story that mattered to her. It was *how* I used the words that counted, not whether or not I knew how to spell them, which would come in time.

I'm not really sure what my mother expected her friend to do with my story. After all, what *could* she do except acknowledge that, yes indeed, it was a story and I had written it. What is particularly memorable about that incident is the picture of my mother hunting out the keys on my father's old portable Smith Corona. She did not know how to type, so it must have taken her hours. Yet it may well have been one of the most important things she ever did for me, because the message she sent was loud and clear. She *liked* what I had written. Someone—someone very special to me and whose opinion mattered a great deal—had approved of my work.

There was no stopping me after that. I took to telling stories, verbally and written, to anyone who would listen. Usually my audience consisted of a few neighborhood friends who sat around looking tolerant while I poured out monster and ghost stories filled with blood and gore. Yes, blood and gore. After all, they were a difficult audience. I did what I had to do to hold their interest. It was one of the first rules I learned. No matter how well crafted, how deeply philosophical, how delightfully metaphorical a story might be, if it didn't entertain, it would flop.

My first "rejection," so to speak, came from my freshman English teacher. I was fourteen. She refused to believe that what I had written was my own work and accused me of stealing someone else's idea. She wasn't sure whose idea, but she was darn sure it wasn't mine. It was a crushing blow. And looking back, I wonder if she ever realized how potentially destructive her accusation had been. It was a paper on which I had worked hard and long. Every word, every thought, had been original. After that incident, I did not share my work with anyone for a long time. At least not until Edith Miles, my English teacher during my junior year, read a story of mine to the class. The story, written for a class assignment, is as vivid in my memory today as it was when I wrote it. The emotion of that moment, the terror of having my work read in front of my peers, has sealed both the moment and the story in my mind forever. The memory is particularly sweet, because it was my first taste of success. Yes, success. Miss Miles and my classmates *liked* what I had written. I was back on track again.

The key word in those previous paragraphs is *audience*. Writers, like all performers, are born to share. I was particularly impressed with Susan Gundlach's article (see page 31) on the subject of creating an audience within the school where children might share their work. And beyond that, creating an atmosphere where students can feel *comfortable* about sharing their writing.

Having a story or poem published is a special occasion. It is the icing on the cake. But the true confirmation during those early years comes from peers, teachers and parents. Every student profiled in the "Young Writers in Print" section of the Guide mentioned the encouragement received from either family members, friends, or teachers. Encouragement from a visible audience may well be the most important ingredient needed to help children through their early struggle to put words on paper.

It was many years before I actually submitted my first manuscript to a publication. When I did, I discovered that not all editors were as gracious as my family had been, nor as tolerant as my neighborhood companions. Still, in spite of the rejection slips—and there were many—my friends and family, and teachers like Miss Miles, had given me a sturdy foundation. I won't pretent that the rejection slips did not hurt. They did. But they did not stop me from writing and submitting my work. Somewhere, deep inside, I knew there were people who did care, who did like my writing. It would be a long, long time before my first book would be published. But the time *did* come. It came because I never gave up. The foundation that had been created in those early years had stood me in good stead.

As I read through the galleys for Kathy Henderson's new edition of the Guide, I couldn't help but wonder if, had I started to approach writing a bit more professionally, earlier on, it might have made a difference. For example, would I have started to submit stories to publications at an earlier age? Would I have published sooner? The fact is, I really don't know. Maybe I would have, maybe not. But one thing is certain. It is a wonderful opportunity for children to have access to such a publication. When they have tested their creations on friends and family; when they have worked hard producing their best stories and poems; they will seek new challenges—bigger and better opportunities. That is as it should be if they are to grow. And when that time comes, I can't think of a better place to begin than right here in the pages of the *Market Guide for Young Writers.*

—Joyce McDonald, President
National Association for Young Writers

A Word to Parents and Teachers

Not every teacher or parent shares my enthusiasm for encouraging young people to attempt publishing. Some argue that the odds are stacked against them; they are too inexperienced. Others fear a rejected manuscript would be too damaging to a child's ego, perhaps turning him or her off writing entirely.

I feel, however, that young people are amazingly resilient. They are constantly seeking new challenges. Given an opportunity they continue to rebound.

We witness this phenomenon each spring as Little Leaguers march up to the plate time and again ever hopeful of getting a meaningful hit. As adults, we consciously guard against letting them give up too quickly.

Shouldn't this philosophy apply to young writers as well as young athletes? Not every Little Leaguer will succeed at the plate, and far fewer still will have Major League careers. Likewise, publishing success cannot be guaranteed for every writer. And only a handful of eager young writers will go on to careers in writing. But in the process, they will be learning valuable skills that will serve them in whatever future career they choose.

It is important to remember that the goal of this Guide is not riches and fame for young writers. Its primary purpose is to provide young writers the opportunity to reach beyond their circle of friends, family and teachers, to explore and share their innermost thoughts, to unleash their imaginations, and to realize the power contained in learning to communicate effectively.

Market Guide for Young Writers was written as much with you in mind as the young people you care about. It is the first of its kind to bring together the wide variety of publications and contests which are especially accessible to writers eighteen and under. Over 300 editors and contest sponsors were queried in regard to their policies, payments, and the potential for young writers to have manuscripts accepted. In addition, many editors and contest sponsors offered specific tips to help young writers get started. The result is a unique collection of over 100 of the best American and Canadian markets available to young people. One Australian magazine is also listed.

Since a young writer needs to know more than just where to send a manuscript, *Market Guide for Young Writers* also contains information on preparing typewritten, handwritten, and computer-printed material for submission. Yet, the entire Guide, with its special charts and easy-to-follow directions, is easy enough for students as young as nine to use on their own.

You will find it just as useful as a reference guide for writers of any age interested in publishing their work.

A special chapter called "Young Writers in Print" provides a wealth of insight and inspiration from eight young people who have already been published. These students, ranging in age from ten to eighteen, come from a variety of backgrounds and have published everything from their own newspapers to hardcover, educational picture books.

Market Guide for Young Writers is the book that I, and many other writers, wish had been available years ago for our own use.

Acknowledgments

The author and publisher of this Guide deeply appreciate the generous cooperation of editors, contest sponsors, and fellow writers who have contributed information and ideas for this edition.

With special thanks to:

THERESA MARIE VALENTINE   SUSAN GUNDLACH

DAVID J. KLEIN   CHRISTINE CLARK

ANNASTASIA L. WORKMAN   RUSSELL BENNETT

CELIA PINSON   SHEILA COWING

AMITY W. GAIGE   MARCIA PRESTON

MIKE SNYDER   CARLA J. CRANE

CINDY SMITH   LINDA HUTTON

DENNIS W. BULGRIEN

CHAPTER ONE

Getting Started

Each month the work of dozens of young writers appears in publications all across the country. To do what these young people have done, you don't need to be at the top of your class in reading or writing, or be labeled "gifted" or "talented." You don't need to know "somebody in the business," have lots of money or years of experience. You don't need to live in an unusual place or lead an unusual life. And you don't need fancy equipment. As many young people have already proven, you don't even need to wait until you are older to try.

There are only two things you do need to know beforehand: *who* publishes the type of material you like to write, and *how* to prepare your finished story, poem, or article before mailing it to an editor or contest. *Market Guide for Young Writers* has that special information plus a lot more to help you become a *Published Young Writer*.

The market and contest lists in this book are the result of a special survey of editors and contest sponsors across the United States and Canada. Their enthusiastic response made it possible to group together a promising list of publications and contests for you to try. Many of the magazines listed have specific sections written entirely by young people. Other magazines, such as those whose readers are mainly adults, are willing to consider the work of young people especially in the areas of essays, opinions, profiles, and personal experience.

Why are so many editors interested in hearing from you? The answer is simple: many of them were once young writers too! One editor expressed the feeling shared by many others when she wrote, "Your guide is a great idea. I only wish it had been available eight or ten years ago for me."

Many of these markets not only publish material from young writers, but offer payment as well. Others offer free copies of issues containing your work instead of payment or sometimes both. As you search through the lists, pay special attention to entries marked with an asterisk (*). Markets and contests bearing this symbol are especially interested in receiving material from young people. They usually have special columns or departments to display your writing and therefore will accept more material from young writers than will other markets.

Please note that a small number of markets and many contests require an entry fee. These listings are marked with a dollar sign ($). They have been included because they either have special sections for young writers or have been known to use a large amount of material written by young people. These markets and contests should be considered only after careful examination. Make sure your material is good enough to make the payment of an entry fee worthwhile.

Give Yourself an Edge

Unfortunately, no one can guarantee that all writers, regardless of age, will find a willing market for their work. However, there are several things you can do to give your material an edge against the competition.

1. Send only your very best work.

Revise and rewrite until each paragraph, sentence, and word says exactly what you mean it to say. Consider asking an adult, perhaps a teacher or parent, to read your manuscript and offer constructive criticism. Listen carefully to their comments, then decide whether you agree or disagree with their advice. Sometimes hearing someone else's opinion will help you to see your material in a new way. Yet always remember that *you* are the creator. You must be the final judge of whether your work is ready to submit. Follow the advice you agree with and politely disregard the rest.

2. Prepare your finished manuscript following the standard formats described in this book.

Occasionally, an editor or contest will want manuscripts to be submitted according to different guidelines. In this case, follow their specific directions.

Many magazines and contests offer tip sheets or writer's guidelines for submitting manuscripts. Take the time to send for these, and follow them as closely as possible. However, in most cases, the standard formats provided here will be acceptable. With few exceptions, these are the same formats used by professional writers.

3. Correct all grammar, punctuation and spelling mistakes in your final copy before mailing.

If you have made only one or two mistakes per page, neatly correct them. There is a list of editing and proofreading marks in this Guide which you can use to make corrections. If you find more mistakes or if your page has a sloppy appearance, take the time to type or handwrite it over one more time. *Then check it again.* This is for your benefit. Since editors cannot meet with you personally and have no idea whether or not you are a good writer, they will judge you by the appearance of your manuscript. By sending a neatly prepared manuscript you will tell editors and contest judges you care enough about what you write to give it the best chance of acceptance.

Think of yourself as a busy editor out to buy a new pair of shoes. Where would you expect to find the best quality? In a store where the shoes are soiled, mismatched and thrown together on a display table for you to sort out? Or in a store where the shoes are neat and clean and paired together for easy selection?

Make it easy for editors and judges to read you material. They will respect the time and effort you have taken. It may well make the difference between an acceptance and a rejection.

4. Study the market and contest information carefully before submitting any manuscript.

There are a number of reasons why editors will reject material regardless of how well written it is. But by far, the biggest and most aggravating reason for rejection is something editors call *inappropriate submission.* This means that that particular publication *never* uses that type of material. The subject of the manuscript may be of little or no interest to the readers. It may be a short story when the publication only uses non-fiction. It may be too long or too short. The wording may be too easy or too hard for the readers. The reasons are many, but in general, they make a manuscript inappropriate for that particular publication.

So take the time to study the market and contest information carefully. Send for and study the guidelines or tip sheets. Buy or send for a sample issue if you are not familiar with the publication. Then read it objectively to determine if your manuscript would fit in.

Pay close attention to the "Editor's Remarks" section of the market listings. Here you will find special advice for submitting material from the editors of several publications. If your manuscript does not meet their requirements, look for a market that does. You might consider rewriting a manuscript to meet the guidelines of a specific market. This is easily done when a manuscript meets most of the requirements but is either a little too long or a little too short, or in the case of a short story, when the main character is too old or too young.

Inappropriate submissions are not only frustrating and time-consuming for the editor, they are a waste of time and postage for you.

5. Understand that an editor may make changes in your manuscript before it appears in print.

Among an editor's responsibilities is the right to revise and correct a writer's manuscript. This is called editing.

Unfortunately, writers don't always agree with the changes an editor makes. We sometimes get mad when an editor rearranges our paragraphs, rewrites some of our sentences, or leaves out parts of our story or article. Still, editors must do what they think is best for their publication.

Try to view any change from the editor's position. If you are still angry, break a few pencils or kick a few wastebaskets until you calm down. Then try to forget what happened to that manuscript and write a new one. Think long and hard before writing or calling an editor to complain. Consider this message from Dawn Brettschneider Korth, former editor of *Straight*:

> "Please tell 'teens' that it's normal to have your work edited. I've had complaints from teen writers when I changed *one word* of a poem—when it was misspelled and used incorrectly! A 16-year-old threatened to sue the company over a poem in which I reversed two lines to make his rhyme scheme consistent. Such scathing letters make editors

reluctant to deal with inexperienced teen writers. All we want to do is help them.''

Many times you'll discover that the changes an editor has made in your manuscript have made it better. If you absolutely *hate* the changes made, do not submit to that market again. There are many other markets from which to choose.

Entering Contests

When entering writing contests, be sure to follow all the stated rules *exactly*. If a contest says you may submit only *one* poem, don't send *two* of your poems. They *both* will probably be disqualified. And you'll lose any money you may have sent for an entry fee without any possibility of winning.

If a contest states entries *must be typed*, be sure to type them. Don't think a judge will overlook the mistakes you make when entering a contest because chances are the judge will never see your entry.

Most contests have a secretary or someone else to open entries and read them to see if the rules have been followed. Only those entries which have followed all the rules will be sent on to the judge or judges.

Don't be a loser before you get started.

Entering contests can be an exciting and rewarding experience. To boost your chances of winning, follow the advice and suggestions below.

1. Send for a complete list of the contest rules, regulations and eligibility requirements.

Unfortunately, space does not allow for all the rules for every contest to be listed in this book. It is best to send a self-addressed stamped envelope (SASE) to receive the rules.

2. Follow all the rules exactly.

This includes where your name, address, and other information are to be placed; the number of entries you may submit; and how manuscripts are to be prepared. If the rules do not give specific guidelines for this information, follow the standard formats provided in this book for submitting manuscripts to an editor.

3. Don't forget to include any entry fees or required forms.

Some contests for young people request that a parent, guardian or teacher include a *signed statement* verifying that the entry has been written entirely by the young person himself. Be sure to include this statement if it is required.

4. Correct all grammar, punctuation and spelling mistakes in your final copy before mailing.

While a judge will be most interested by what you say in your writing, he will also be impressed with neatness. You should be proud enough of your work to polish it to perfection.

5. Don't limit yourself to contests designed just for young writers.

Many talented young writers have placed or won in contests open to adults. However, you have the best chance of winning in contests open to young people only.

6. If possible, try to read the winning entries of an annual contest from the previous year.

Just as reading back issues of magazines will help you understand an editor's viewpoint, so will studying past winners of a contest. Yet, don't let this stop you from entering something original and different.

7. Don't be discouraged if you don't win.

Most contests award prizes for only first, second and third place. Some also name a number of honorable mention winners. A judge, like you, has his personal likes and dislikes. Out of the many entries, a judge must choose only a few, and he will make his selection according to what he likes best. Another judge, or editor, may like your work better.

A Word About Rejection

Becoming a *Published Young Writer* takes more than enthusiasm and talent. You must also be aware of the opportunities. You must be willing to study and follow the guidelines set by editors and contest sponsors. You must understand that while some manuscripts are rejected for poor writing, others are rejected for reasons not readily apparent to the writer. These include: the time needed by a publication to print an issue, the space available for printing manuscripts, how many manuscripts are received for consideration, the number of manuscripts which have already been accepted for publication, and the personal preferences of the editors, staff, and judges.

Rejection is disappointing. It hurts.

But rejection must be put in perspective. The editor or judge has not rejected *you* personally. He has simply picked someone else's manuscript which better suited his needs at that moment—much like you might consider one pair of shoes over another of equal quality.

You should feel especially honored if an editor or judge sends back any advice, comments or criticism about your manuscript.

Editors are busy people who deal with hundreds of manuscripts each year. They cannot afford either the time or expense to write to you personally about why your manuscript was rejected. Most times you will receive a generic, preprinted note known as the *form rejection slip.*

The wording on a form rejection is usually so vague it is difficult to tell exactly why a manuscript was rejected. There is, however, an unofficial code many editors use to signal writers that their manuscript has some merit. It is a busy editor's way of offering encouragement. The code goes something like this:

If an editor *signs* his name, then something in your manuscript caught his eye. It may be the flow of your words, your ability to make a point, your characterization within a story, or something else. You are on the right track. Keep at it!

If an editor *jots a word or two of encouragement*, such as "good idea" or "nice try," he means your manuscript was better than most but perhaps lacked that certain spark that would have made it outstanding. Give it another try.

If an editor *writes a few words of advice or criticism*, such as "your characters are a little weak" or "the plot needs tightening up," he means your manuscript was good enough to be given careful consideration. With a little more effort, you probably have a winner.

Of course, there are variations on this code. Some editors try hard to encourage promising young writers and will send a short, personal note rather than a rejection slip. Others simply do not have the time to spare. And sometimes a rejection slip that simply says, "Sorry. This does not fit our needs at this time," means just that. They can't use it whether or not they like it.

Rather than dreading a bit of criticism, look forward to it eagerly. It is usually easier to pinpoint minor flaws in a well-written manuscript than in a poorly-written one where the trouble is so spread out. It is hard to offer any meaningful help in a short note. An editor who takes the time to offer encouragement, either by praise or constructive criticism, deserves your appreciation. Whether you make use of that advice is up to you.

You may be lucky enough to find yourself a *Published Young Writer* with your first attempt. Then again, you may need to submit material many times before, finally, one of your manuscripts is selected for publication. Never be discouraged. With practice your writing will get better and better, and so will your chances of being published.

Be careful not to set the wrong goals for yourself. A writer whose only goal is to be published will likely experience many more disappointments than will a writer who hopes to be published one day but whose goal is to enjoy writing and become a better writer.

It is unrealistic to expect everything you write to win a contest or be accepted for publication. Consider how a musician prepares for a performance.

He may continue to take lessons, trying out new pieces, practicing over and over again pieces he has learned in the past. For his actual performance, he will not play every piece he has practiced. Instead he will pick and choose those he plays the best. He also considers which pieces he feels the audience will like hearing.

As a writer, your audience is your reader; your performance, your manuscript. Pick and choose manuscripts you feel represent your best work. And when choosing which markets and contests to submit to, consider what would interest the readers of those publications.

Take the time now to turn to the special chapter called "Young Writers in Print." There you will find profiles of eight young writers ranging in age from ten to eighteen who have already had material published. Listen carefully to what they have to say. Their experience may help you.

The "Editors Are Real People Too" chapter will introduce you to seven editors and contest sponsors and will give you a behind-the-scenes look into what they look for in the manuscripts they select. Their helpful advice and suggestions can be applied to submitting your work to other markets and contests as well.

I'd like to hear about you and your experiences as a young writer. Perhaps I'll include a profile of you in the next edition of Market Guide for Young Writers. *Send your letters, questions and comments to me at 2151 Hale Road, Sandusky, Michigan 48471.*

CHAPTER TWO

Young Writers in Print

Theresa Marie Valentine

Theresa Valentine, ten, lives in Mission Viejo, California, with her mother and little brother Davy. Her bubbly personality shows through in her writing, making it seem as if she's speaking right to you. Though she has won a couple writing contests, having her first submitted story accepted was an experience she'll never forget.

Theresa wants to be a rich and famous writer by the time she's thirteen. A tall order for a ten year old. But with her motivation and determination, Theresa just might do it.

When I think about it, it seems like I have been writing forever, but I never really planned on trying to become published; it just sort of happened. I was always fascinated with the English language. Mom says I never said things like "Ma Ma" and "Da Da" when I was a baby. She says I just opened my mouth and started speaking in paragraphs!

I can remember Mom reading to me when I was really tiny. Poor Mom. I was always begging her to read to me. When she had to be doing other things, I remember looking at the books and being really frustrated and disappointed that I couldn't understand the printed words myself. I decided to learn to read as soon as I could.

My family remembers that I had been in school only a few weeks when I was able to zoom through the little books they give you when you are just learning to read. I really give credit to my first-grade teacher, Sister Breda Christopher. She was the best teacher I have ever had.

I used to read my mom's poetry volumes and encyclopedias. When I would ask questions such as, "Why is the grass green?" my mother would never never tell me she didn't know. Instead she would stop what she was doing and help me look up the answer. Then we would spend hours flipping through the encyclopedia.

In first grade I concentrated on learning to read and write. In second grade I won a statewide competition for a poem I wrote about Father Serra, the founder of many California Missions. In third grade I won a nationwide competition for an essay about the Statue of Liberty for her re-dedication. I loved to write plays and drove my little brother Davy nuts because I would be the director and make him act out the scenes and make the words on the paper come to life.

This past year, fourth grade, was really the turning point. We moved to a new community and I found myself attending public school for the first time. I was tested for the GATE (Gifted and Talented Education) program. Mom called the school district and asked about the program and they told her that it centered on language arts—right up my alley! We studied poetry: jingles, limericks and haiku. They were so easy for me that I could write pages and pages at a time. One time a volunteer teacher asked me if I was copying them from a book. I couldn't understand how she could ask me that when she could see that I was sitting right there in front of her while writing them!

There was a local talent contest coming up. Everyone in my family is creative in some way, so they all wanted to enter. My grandma is a costume designer. She makes all the costumes for our family's party business. My Aunt Chrissie is a gifted artist. My Uncle Bejan is a drummer in a band. My other aunt, GiGi, is a singer, dancer, model and actress. She holds the state title of California Teen Miss Charm 1987-88. My mother dabbles in writing herself. (My dad died when I was two.) And my little brother Davy is cute no matter what he does. So I figured that if I wanted to enter this contest, I had better find something I was good at, and the only thing I could think of was writing. So I wrote a story about my puppy. Most of it was quite true, but I admit I spiced it up a bit by adding a little fiction. I didn't win the contest because they really had no category for my entry, but many people told me afterward how great my story was.

My mom said that it was good enough to be published but she really didn't know where to send it. We found *Market Guide for Young Writers* and sent the story to a few places. And it was accepted! Now I'm on my way. The newspaper came out and gave me a wonderful interview, and I have lots of other ideas for more writing. I am collecting my poetry right now for submission, and I am planning something really exciting—an advice column for kids! Now all I have to do is get a local paper interested in the idea.

That's about it—not really exciting, yet. But after all, I'm only ten. I intend to be a rich and famous author by the time I'm thirteen. Mom says I can do it. And I say I will!

David J. Klein

David J. Klein, ten, of Akron, Ohio, is a very friendly and open fourth grader who is evidently proud of his accomplishment in winning the Raintree Publish-a-Book Contest but hasn't let it go to his head. David has one brother, Adam, who is twenty months older. He asked Adam to read his story at the awards ceremony so they both could share in the limelight.

Getting to the winner's circle wasn't easy for David. When his teacher, Diane Koltnow, directed her English class to write a story for the Akron Board of Education's Young Authors' Program, David waited until the last minute to begin the assignment. His Irwin the Sock *was born in tears of frustration and panic. His mother helped him get his story on paper. "Once he came upon the idea," says Linda Klein, "I played secretary for him because I didn't want him further frustrated by not being able to get the words down right. I prompted him with questions like what else happens to socks or what did the character do next?"*

Although the names "Irwin" and "Irma" have no special significance, many aspects of David's story relate to his family, friends and personal experiences. For instance, David's grandfather, to whom the book is dedicated, was a broker of textile machinery and dealt with many factories in New England.

David comes from a background of creative writers. His father is a sports editor for the Lansing State Journal *in Michigan. His mother, a financial planner and tax consultant, has done some public relations writing. And one of David's grandparents was a poet.*

David has some special memories about winning the book contest.

We had Raintree posters everywhere. Our teacher, Ms. Koltnow, made writing a book an assignment. Everyone had to do it.

I got more interested everyday after we found out someone from from our school had placed. But for three days our teacher wouldn't say who had placed or where. We kids were very disappointed and said we wouldn't do our work unless she gave us a hint. Finally she said that it was one of the boys. All the girls moaned. All the boys yelled and jumped up from their seats.

I like writing, though I mostly only do it for school. I like to read more than write, especially mysteries, science fiction, and interesting non-fiction about sports.

I'm not sure what I'd like to be in the future. I used to say a dirt biker but that's not very practical. Whatever it is, I want it to have a good paycheck!

Annastasia L. Workman

Twelve-year-old Annastasia Workman of Great Falls, Montana, says she wrote her first story when she was only two years old. Now she writes and publishes her own magazine. She would like other young writers to consider submitting material for her magazine. She currently has ten subscribers and sells her Rainbow Magazine *for thirty cents. Annastasia would also like to have pen pals to write to. Address pen pal letters or magazine submissions to: Annastasia Workman, 1200 32nd Street South L96, Great Falls, MT 59405. Don't forget to include a self-addressed stamped envelope for her to use to respond to you the first time.*

I composed my first poem when I was five years old. I wrote my first real story shortly after that. The spelling was phonetic so it was hard to read.

I have entered poetry contests in *Cricket* since I was nine. I received one honorable mention and a stack of rejection slips. This did not encourage me to go on writing very much. I do well in language, reading and spelling. That helps my writing.

When my brother first got a job shoveling snow and got paid $3.50 per hour, I was jealous. I looked for ways to earn money, too. My parents and I decided that I could write a magazine and sell it to them. My magazine was called *Vista Cruiser, U.S.A.* At first I only sold it to my parents. Then I expanded and took subscriptions. The magazine was written by hand and Xeroxed. In 1985, my mom gave me her old typewriter. With it, I wrote *Muddy Pickup, U.S.A.* and *Rainbow Magazine* in addition to *Vista Cruiser, U.S.A.* Now I use a Commodore 64 to do my magazine. I use the program called "Newsroom," which my sixth-grade teacher, Mr. Rickert, suggested when my mom told him about my magazine. Soon, I plan to use our Amiga computer to do my magazine. I will use the program "Pagesetter."

Right now, my *Rainbow Magazine* is a weekly magazine. Soon, I plan to make it a bigger and better monthly magazine.

My grandma entered one of my poems in the Jackson Regional Library Literary Competition. I won first place in my age group (kindergarten – eighth grade). I received a fifteen dollar check, a ribbon, a certificate, and an invitation to the opening of the library. It was very exciting.

I get a lot of encouragement at school and at home to go on with my writing. When Mr. Rickert said I could help kids with "Newsroom" for the school paper, I was very pleased.

My current interest in writing could affect me in the future because, since I write so much now, I do well in language arts classes. My language grades might make a difference in which school or college I go to. I think I'm better at piano than writing, so I don't think I'll make a career in writing.

Some advice I'd give to other students interested in publishing their own material and submitting to magazines and contests is: Keep working hard and don't give up. When submitting to magazines or contests, always write to the editor of the magazine or contest to get detailed information.

Celia Pinson

Celia Pinson, twelve, is a seventh grade student at The Savannah Country Day School in Savannah, Georgia. She plunged into publishing the way most students her age raid the refrigerator after school. She has many publishing credits to show for her efforts.

A bookworm for years, Celia feels her love of reading sparked her interest in writing. Editor Gerry Mandel of Stone Soup *calls Celia "a very serious and talented writer."*

I have been producing creative writings for over seven years and my writing interests are varied. When I was eight, I began sending collections of my stories to special friends and relatives as Christmas gifts. I did this for three years until my stories became more lengthy. When I turned eleven, I began sending out a bimonthly newsletter to over ninety people who had specifically asked to be on my mailing list. Each newsletter, entitled *Selections from Celia's Pen*, included one of my latest stories.

At nine, I received my first formal recognition as a writer when my school participated in a city-wide essay contest. I had quite a time writing that essay and had no idea anything would ever come of it. The winners were announced while my family and I were traveling in England. When I returned to school, I was surprised to see many of my classmates waiting for me at the door. As soon as I appeared, they all began talking at once. I finally grasped what they were trying to tell me. I had won the essay contest!

When I was ten, I set up a sidewalk shop in a little nook beneath the front stoop of my nineteenth-century townhouse, which is located on a busy tour route in the heart of Savannah's historic district. Since it was late October, I decided to try selling a witch story I had written. For forty-five cents, a copy of my story could be purchased and my customers also received a complimentary cup of "Wanda Warlocker lemonade." My little sister, Melissa, dressed up like Wanda Warlocker (the name of the witch in my story) and acted as my agent. She was terrific! When I closed my shop a few hours later, we had sold all thirty-five copies and had been photographed by a newspaper photographer. A picture of Melissa and me sitting next to my shop, "The Dungeon," appeared in color on the feature page of *The Savannah Morning News* the day before Halloween.

A few months after my experience at "The Dungeon," I was selected to be one of several students featured on a local television station's "Young and Successful Students" series. It was neat being interviewed about something I enjoyed so much, to see myself, and to hear excerpts from some of my stories on TV.

My church, the Independent Presbyterian Church, has supported me in my writing pursuits since I was nine years old. I was asked at that time to write a Christmas story for publication in the church's annual Advent booklet. Since then, I have been asked to make other contributions through my writing for various church projects and programs. There is now an area in the church library designated as "Celia's Corner" where a large collection of my writings is kept. Because of this support and my realization that writing is a God-given gift, it was especially meaningful for me to have my first published magazine piece appear in *Clubhouse*, a national Christian publication. It was a poem and has since been published in two newspapers, a national writer's newsletter, and accepted for publication in another Christian magazine for teens.

During the past year, I have won and been a finalist in several local and national writing contests. I have also had poems and stories accepted for publication in five different national magazines and have been asked to write two articles for a teenage tabloid. Based on an essay, I was selected to serve for a year on the Student Advisory Board for *Gifted Children Monthly*. Recently my teachers chose me to be the first recipient of our school's "Anne Frank Writing Award." I feel it is the climax of my recognition as a writer so far.

Another memorable experience happened when one of my former Lower School teachers asked me to read some of my stories to students. Over a period of eight days, I read to six groups, discussed my stories with them and answered their questions. I was so surprised when I received a batch of letters from the students. Some even drew pictures of my characters and some sent along stories they had written. It was an experience I will never forget. I've also been invited twice to local libraries to read my stories for special programs.

After I complete my education, I want to be a professional author/illustrator and a first or second-grade school teacher.

I urge young writers not to become discouraged if they receive a rejection. I feel if a writer believes that he or she has a publishable work, then different markets should be pursued until one is found that accepts it. When I was eleven, I wrote a tribute to my father and submitted it to a local newspaper for their Father's Day issue but they didn't accept it. Instead of letting it get me down, I submitted it to a national magazine for children and it was accepted. The tribute appeared the next year in the Father's Day issue of *Stone Soup* along with an illustration which I drew at their request. This experience just shows what I believe: God never closes a window without opening a door.

Amity W. Gaige

Amity Gaige, fifteen, of Reading, Pennsylvania, has a publishing history that goes all the way back to 1982 when she won third place in the Cricket *League poetry contest for five to nine year olds. Other credits include such diverse publications as* Reading Eagle *and* Reading Times, *Waldenbooks* Kids' Club Magazine, Merlyn's Pen, Pathways *and* Shoe Tree.

Amity sees a close relationship between psychology and the arts and feels the world would be a more peaceful place if people were encouraged to write, rather than act, out their feelings.

I believe that writing is one of the highest forms of self-expression. It falls into the same category as music, dance, studio art and theater, all of which I also love.

Psychology and the arts have always been of interest to me because they are so closely connected to writing. If only angry people would write, sing or dance their feelings, the world would be so much more peaceful. That's how my career began, as an angry child who was told by my mother to "write my feelings down." So, instead of throwing a temper tantrum like other little kids, I'd purse my lips and mutter my way to the study where I'd sit tiny in my chair and scratch "I Hate Mommy and Daddy" stories. They are now kept in a dusty folder; thin yellow documents of my juvenile rage that now make me laugh.

Whenever I was upset with people, I'd write a hate story. It would go like this one, "I hate my Mommy and Daddy. When they thinck they know something I know its rong. When we went to the zoo My Mommy and Daddy dident know an anmol and I did it was a peeckock ya! and when we went to the mouseeem they did not know who was the famus printer I did it was Shacksspeer." That's how it all began.

Because of the anti-TV atmosphere in my home, I learned to do more creative things. Even before I learned to write, I loved to create skits. Later on, I wrote scripts and produced, directed and starred in my own plays. I'd have my friends be supporting actors, and their names would always appear smaller than mine on the mock play bills. I wrote plays for my third, fifth and sixth-grade classes, and we put them on for the school.

I used to love to sing at my mother's friend's recording studio. My sister would sit in the booth and record the improvised songs that I'd croon a cappella with the headphones hanging off my head like two big kaiser rolls.

Being a creative child wasn't all fantasy. There was a looming reality unknown to me, and that reality was "The Average Person." I figured everybody did the weird things I did, and everyone would appreciate me. Then came my first-grade teacher. She was the first adult, other than my parents, to whom I showed my writing. I still remember the piece. It was called the "Flat Mat." I had intended it as a friendly gesture to say, "See what I can do!" But she gave back my paper with red circles around all my misspellings and added, "Please watch your spelling." She was probably just a hunched over purple-haired lady, but time has distorted her into a thin, warty witch with black whip-like hair. After all, I was so shattered that I didn't show my work to anybody else for at least a year. But bad finally balanced with good when my second-grade teacher had me illustrate the "Flat Mat" and make it into a little booklet to show to the class.

I especially remember Madeline Tiger Bass. She was a poet who came into our third-grade class on a grant from the National Endowment for the Humanities to introduce the kids to poetry, and she paid special attention to me. She included one of my poems in her final report to the school district, and she wrote, "If it's possible to identify talent at this early age, this is it." I remember how she kept my spelling of "above" as "obove." Even though I really didn't know how to spell it, she said it was part of the poem and the spelling made it even more mine. I was lucky to have contact with someone like that. I hope she's still out there.

After that, my father began taking my writing more seriously, researching contests and publishing opportunities in children's magazines. I began to win prizes and be published. I owe much of my rapid progress to my parents, especially my father who spends much time typing, photocopying and mailing for me.

My parents looked for writing classes for me. They found an adult class at a local school for the arts. The teacher, Barbara Chimochowski, has now become my private writing teacher and has helped me to publish my work. My parents also encouraged me to apply to the Johns Hopkins University Center for the Advancement of Academically Talented Youth, and for the last two summers I have participated in the Center's wonderful writing program, which has been invaluable to me. I am lucky my parents even care that I write, let alone go out of their way for me. Many potential writers have probably been squelched by parents who neglected to water them and just let them wilt.

I'll always write. Even if my life had been full of purple-haired first grade teachers, I'd still be writing. Becoming a professional writer is my dream, but I'd also like to travel around the world for a few years. I've wanted to do that all my life. It is hard to think of anything more inspiring to a writer than the vista from the Himalayan mountains under a silent shivering blue sky, or the transparent green Caribbean Sea reflecting the sun like a thousand prisms.

As I grow older, I become even more grateful for the people who have been genuinely interested in my writing. I am also grateful for the talent that makes me want to do more than just scratch out another tired verse of roses are red, violets are blue. I see it this way. Some people put me on TV. Some people put me down. Some people say "That's genius." And some people say, "Oh, nice." But the fact is that I know I love to write, and what other people think is far less important than what I know.

Mike Snyder

Mike Snyder of Allen, Oklahoma, was first profiled in the 1986-87 edition of Market Guide for Young Writers *when he was twelve years old. At that time, he had already written more than 200 stories but had only been published a few times in the local newspaper. Mike had also made copies of some of his stories and sold them himself to friends and family. Though most of his family encouraged him, one of Mike's brothers and a lot of his friends thought he was just wasting his time by writing so much. That didn't stop him, though. Mike continued to write and explore publishing opportunities even expanding his self-publishing projects.*

Three years later, after some publishing success in national markets, Mike says his friends are more respectful of his desire to write and publish. He still gets rejection slips but regards them as tools which can help him write better stories in the future.

Since I was profiled in the first edition of *Market Guide*, things have really changed. I have had three items published, a non-fiction article, a maze and a cartoon. All were published by *Creative Kids* magazine.

I can't express the feeling of joy and pride I felt when I read the acceptance letters. They seemed to say, "What you created is good enough to be shared with thousands of readers." There was no payment of money and, of course, none was needed. Getting to see my work in a magazine was worth more than money. The accompanying feeling can't be replaced.

A collection of my stories will be appearing in *Connections, Volume II*. Although a fee of twenty-five dollars was required, it was worth it. Since my works have been published, the skeptics at school aren't as skeptical anymore. When I'm older I will probably write for money. Until then, just being in print will satisfy me.

Of course, that isn't *everything* that has happened. I have also received many rejection slips. The editors are usually gentle with rejections. In most cases, I've gotten suggestions and warm comments from them. Rejections aren't something to fear; they simply help a manuscript have a better chance at the next market.

Many young writers have a collection of stories they wrote when they were younger. I'm no exception. Many of these stories have inspired me to write better versions to submit to markets. Some are even good enough to use the entire story (after careful editing!). Never think that writing is a waste of time. Even for those who don't want to be published, creative writing is a valuable thing.

Kids interested in writing should get a pen pal. Continuously writing your feelings and what goes on during everyday life can improve how you express things. It also provides this opportunity for another person. One such magazine that contains pen pal information is *Creative Kids*.

In March 1985, I began to publish and sell a mini-magazine called *The Runaways*. Then in March of 1987, I created *Stargazer*, a one-page daily newspaper containing stories and puzzles. I went a step farther than I had with *The Runaways* by allowing my classmates to contribute items.

My English teacher, Miss Lindley, was always a source of inspiration. She wanted me to compile and publish a book of stories. Many of my friends and classmates were contributing items. I had just begun to edit the material when I broke my arm. Without its use, I had to hunt and peck on the typewriter and eventually abandoned the project because by the time my six-week healing period was over, so was school.

The fourth, and hopefully final, stage in my publishing company evolution is MBC which stands for Mini Books Company. MBC will publish stories on almost any subject in the form of small twelve-page books written by writers ages eight to sixteen. Submissions are limited to 1,000 words. Young writers interested in more details can send a self-addressed stamped envelope to: MBC, c/o Mike Snyder, Route 2, Box 81, Allen, OK 74825.

Cindy Smith

Cindy Smith of Wichita, Kansas, was a junior in high school when she placed fourth in Guideposts *Youth Writing contest and won a $3,000 scholarship.*

For Cindy, the process of writing is an emotional journey which, though she travels willingly, is still strewn with ruts and tangles. She longs to be the kind of writer who can compose first-draft masterpieces. But she's learning she can overcome any writing problem she encounters with perseverance and occasional professional assistance.

To me, writing is a void, a void within myself in which no boundaries exist. Into this void I can escape thus filling it with emotions: frustration, pain, sorrow, hope, contentment, or enchantment. Writing provides me with unlimited freedom—freedom to express my opinions, to challenge myself with unending possibilities. Although I have always felt comfortable with writing, it has not always been easy to compose a "well-written" piece.

As a young child, I was inspired by my sister's creative ability to write poetry. As long as I can remember, my wish has been to be considered a talented writer, someone like my sister who can sit down and immediately produce a quality piece. This experience has never been within my reach. Often times I have significant trouble finding adequate words with which to express myself. As I get older, I find this to be increasingly difficult. Yet, I have also discovered my abilities to be greater. For instance, with each stuggle I have had, I have been able to find a solution. I have learned to broaden my vocabulary thus providing my writing with more depth. There are many advantages to using sources such as the thesaurus and the dictionary to achieve desired effects. Frequently relying on one's own resources for the creative way of expressing oneself will only bring about frustration.

There is great advantage to obtaining help from someone who is experienced in writing or English skills. It can be difficult to find the proper way, grammatically, to express one's thoughts. Writing is spontaneous. Feelings and opinions are often communicated with very little thought to the use of correct form. In numerous incidents I have written a sentence with much meaning and emotion, then had to change it because of incorrect grammar. An experienced person in these matters can be of great help to show a foiled writer how to convey his ideas and at the same time be grammatically correct.

Discouragement is a common emotional experience in a young writer's life. There can be periods during which one is very active with his writing and, likewise, periods when activity has ceased. Perhaps the words will not come to mind, or a finished piece is not up to one's own expectations. The key to this mental block is repetition. One cannot achieve if one does not make an attempt at his goal. Setting down ideas for personal writing goals can be a good substitute when the words themselves are scarce. This can be the tool to "get the ball rolling" to a successful writing experience.

My experience with writing has been very fulfilling. I have found writing to have a great many faces; each one depends on my imagination and mood at the time. If a young writer has dreams of a career in a related field, he must never stop trying to discover new faces. When writing is an enjoyment, this task can turn into a wonderful adventure.

To me, writing is a void with no boundaries. Perhaps to another young writer it is a selfless companion. In any case, writing is unrestrained, and only writing can be expanded to fit any individual's needs. This is true freedom.

Dennis W. Bulgrien

Dennis Bulgrien, eighteen, is a senior at Sandusky High School located in the upper "thumb" region of Michigan. He feels his love of reading — fantasy in particular — led him to test his own hand at writing. After receiving 4-H honors for two of his short stories, Dennis then entered them in a regional writer's club contest even though he knew he would be competing with adult writers.

Though Dennis doesn't plan on pursuing a writing career, he approaches his writing, nonetheless, with a good deal of professionalism, realizing how rewriting and revising can improve a story.

My parents were missionaries in South-Central Africa. I was born where they were stationed and my education for first and second grades was in Adastra Primary School, a Zambian government school. Creative writing was not taught; in fact, English was taught by a national who only knew English as a second language. My parents, my two brothers, and I came back to the United States when I was eight.

While I was in Africa, and during the years following our return to the States, I never thought of writing as anything other than an assignment. For whatever reason, spelling and English grammar have always been difficult for me.

I had taken a creative writing class in sixth grade but little came of it. I cannot remember any stories from my English classes that were exceptional until my junior year in high school. That year Mr. Schumacher, my English teacher, assigned a lot of writing. He would designate a theme and we were allowed to choose the writing style. I frequently chose to write fantasy stories, probably because I liked reading fantasies. Two of my favorite authors are J.R.R. Tolkien and David Eddings. My experiences in Africa may have heightened my fascination in that area because of the mysticism and witchcraft.

On one occasion, Mr. Schumacher assigned the theme "If all people in the world looked physically alike, how would I know myself?" I used Dickens's idea of spirits, recalling scenes from my past, to portray my morals and personality. Mr. Schumacher was so impressed that he had it printed in our local newspaper, the *Sandusky Tribune*. That recognition really encouraged me to make writing more than just an assignment. It is an extension of myself which portrays what kind of person I am. My ideals inevitably show through and hopefully will make an impact on those who read my work.

After that first accomplishment, I wrote two other fantasy stories each approximately 1,500 words long. Whenever I sit down to write, I have my *Merriam-Webster Dictionary* and *Webster's New World Thesaurus* at my side. They are good tools for improving style and making use of word variety which help convey the same feelings and emotions the writer wishes to relate. After all, that is what writing is all about.

No matter how hard someone tries to write a perfect paper, there are almost always points which can be improved or clarified. Having someone else read a paper helps me recognize ambiguous portions. When I gave the stories to Mom for proofreading, she found places where the events were distorted and unclear. I had not noticed them since I was writing the story and had the situation in my mind.

After numerous rough drafts, I thought my stories must be flawless. I submitted the stories as 4-H County Fair creative writing projects and received a blue ribbon on each as well as a County Honor for my short story "Fantasy."

When I heard about the Thumb Area Writer's Club Spring Writing Contest, I entered my two stories and a poem. After that, I went back through the stories and, to my surprise, was able to improve the wording so as to bring my ideas across even better. After the fair, I received a notice from TAWC that I had received an award for one of my entries. When I attended Awards Night, I found out that one of my stories, "Consequences," got honorable mention and "Fantasy" took first. Although I did get prize money for first place, having my story printed in the TAWC newsletter *Thumbprints* will be far more rewarding.

Sometimes I have to think about what I want to write long beforehand. When I think of a situation or see a scene that arouses emotion, I write it down in a special note pad set aside for such ideas. Sometimes I do not put an idea in my note pad and later, no matter how hard I try, I am unable to remember all the spectacular ideas that I had thought of earlier.

Although I enjoy writing, I doubt that I will make it a career. However, I am learning valuable skills for the future. Writing ability can be employed in so many ways. For example, I enjoy programming text adventure computer games. Text adventures are role playing games where the player becomes the main character and acts out his or her own story by giving the computer commands which tell it what the character is attempting to do. This summer I completed one named *Nuka Hiva* in which the player takes the role of a pirate mutineer who is forced to walk the plank. He swims to a nearby island with an active volcano, Nuka Hiva, and must find a way to escape before the volcano erupts and destroys everything alive. I have started another one based on a role-playing adventure book, *Lone Wolf.* Computer programming is a good area to get into now, and with the opportunity to write as well as program, it seems an even better idea for me.

CHAPTER THREE

Editors Are Real People Too

Unless you have an editor for a mother or father and know firsthand that they're ordinary people who break the yolk flipping their breakfast eggs and drip jelly from their toast just like everyone else, editors can seem a mysterious lot. It's hard to get to know one when the only place you meet is through the pages of a publication.

Yet, most editors are an energetic, friendly group. Many started out as young writers and have experienced the same frustrations and thrills you experience trying to capture word pictures on paper. In this chapter, a new addition to *Market Guide for Young Writers*, you'll have a chance to meet seven editors who make encouraging young writers a priority.

In their own words, they'll share a bit of personal history, advice for submitting to their publication, and/or explain how they came to sponsor special writing contests for young people. They represent a variety of top-notch publishing opportunities for students.

Once you meet them, we hope you'll agree editors are not only real people, but nice ones, too.

Susan Gundlach
Teacher at North Shore Country Day School

As students, your first contact with editors and the editorial process will be through your own teachers. And just as editors at publishing houses come in a variety of editorial personalities, from responsive and super-encouraging to aloof and heavy-handed, teachers, too, differ in their interest and approach to creative writing and their interaction with their students. Many professional writers give credit for their success to the encouragement and direction given by a former teacher. Other writers, like Amity Gaige, survived unpleasant experiences with a less-than-sensitive teacher and had to draw upon their own determination to carry them through.

Susan Gundlach is a teacher at North Shore Country Day School in Winnetka, Illinois, near Chicago. At North Shore, creative writing isn't just an elective course or one squeezed into a regular language arts program, it is an integral and complimentary part of the overall curriculum. A highlight of their program is the wide variety of in-school publishing opportunities offered to students. While North Shore stresses in-school publishing, Ms. Gundlach and other teachers also offer help to students who want to pursue outside publishing opportunties. Here, Ms. Gundlach gives an inside look at the benefits of in-school writing opportunites for students.

> Picture a lovely brown mansion with vines growing up the neglected walls. The lifeless house is scary, but beckoning. I see myself as a little girl about nine or ten, wearing a blue sailor dress, white knee-high socks, and shiny shoes. I have blonde, bouncy, curly hair pulled back from my face, and a hat covers the top of my head . . .
>
> *—from* "The Dream" *by Amy Jacobs, 8th grade*

In the front hallway of the Upper School at North Shore Country Day is a bulletin board headed "Published Artists Among Us," displaying many of the stories, poems, essays, and drawings our students have had accepted by literary magazines that feature children's work. More than fifty students from our small K–12 school have been published over the past year and a half. Amy, author of "The Dream," even received letters from students in New Jersey who read her story and wanted to comment on it and ask her questions.

We are proud of our young writers. They and their teachers have worked hard to achieve such success. However, I have found that we have to be careful not to get too carried away with publishing fever, attractions of celebrity notwithstanding. It is important to examine, every so often, the value of publishing and to place it in proper perspective. What is publishing; what does it mean to students, and why should we as teachers promote it?

Right away the issue becomes complicated, for there are at least two categories of publishing: (1) within the school in various forms, and (2) outside of school through the kinds of magazines listed in the *Market Guide for Young Writers*. Although the two activities are both called publishing, they are, in fact, not interchangeable. At North Shore we see the first category as a key part of the writing process—after students work at planning, drafting, and revising, they are ready to "make public" what they have written. Publishing within the school provides opportunities for student writers to communicate with a responsive audience and for students to participate in an active community of writers.

We construe the term "publishing" broadly to cover all kinds of sharing; so, for example, students who read their compositions aloud in class are engaged in one type of publishing. Other means of sharing might include writing conferences with the teacher and/or peers, programs presented to parents or other classes in the school, bulletin board displays, and booklets and magazines created by individuals or larger groups of students. Through these kinds of activities, young writers are able to gain the satisfaction of sharing their writing soon after it is completed. One third grader brought down the house at an all-school assembly when he read a limerick he had written:

> There once was a miner named Piner.
> He was hungry and went to the diner.
> He had roast beef,
> And he said to the chief,
> "No diner could ever be finer!"
> — *Morgan Campbell*

Not great literature, but a great moment for the author.

Most writers at any grade level appreciate not only enthusiastic ovations but also quiet, considered responses from their teachers and classmates: "I like the way you describe your grandfather;" "The sound imagery in line three is very effective;" "Why did you use this particular phrase to lead into your conclusion?" In-school publishing, with the reactions and discussions it elicits, is a powerful way of conveying to students that what they have to say is important. Serious, careful attention to writing helps mold the class, or the school as a whole, into a community that values reading and writing. At North Shore this kind of sharing is an integral part of the writing process, for every student deserves to have his/her writing read (or heard) and responded to.

Fortunately, the vast majority of magazines that solicit student writing are run by people who do show respect for young writers. As a teacher I enjoy working along with such magazines, and I find that they provide a nice supplement to the kinds of publishing we already do at our school. Recently, I spoke with a former student who had had an essay accepted for publication when he was a senior in high school. His reflections on the experience reinforce some of my own observations and present some new ideas as well. He said that when the essay was first completed, his teacher read it aloud to several of her classes, and afterwards "kids came up to me and told me they liked certain parts." Looking back, he thought that in some ways, these responses had been more significant than publication in a magazine. "Perhaps it's more important to hear from friends who liked my writing; it's closer to home." On the other hand, he said it was "really exciting" to see his work in print. He found that he gained a fresh perspective on his own writing partly because his piece appeared so long after he had actually written it, and partly because he could read it in the context of the other material in the magazine. He added that this early exposure to publishing would serve him well should he ever want to write for publication again. He now knows he could do it.

By taking a realistic view of out-of-school publishing, and at the same time emphasizing in-class sharing of written work, teachers can offer their students the benefits of both kinds of publishing. The few lucky students who succeed with outside publication can and should enjoy the honor they have won, but we must also keep in mind that all young writers need, as well, encouragement, approbation, and advice from friends and teacher/editors closer to home.

Christine Clark
Editor at Children's Better Health Institute

Christine Clark is the current editor of Humpty Dumpty *magazine aimed at readers four to six years old. She has been with the Children's Better Health Institute for several years and has been editor or associate editor for a number of their magazines. Here, she shares her own early beginnings as a writer and tips for submitting material to all CBHI publications.*

Somewhere in my attic there's a big box filled with spiral notebooks. The notebooks are filled with stories and poems that I wrote when I was a child. Writing was one of my favorite pastimes.

At first, I was shy about letting anyone read my stories and poems. They seemed so private and personal. But one day I showed my parents a funny story I had written about my dog, Raisin. They laughed and thought my story was great! So I read a story about a sick little boy to my younger sisters. They felt sad and asked me to write more stories about the little boy. In grade school, a teacher read a spy story of mine out loud to the class. Some friends said that they wished they could write exciting stories like mine.

Well! From that time on, writing was very different for me. It was still something I did in private because I liked to do it, but it also took on a new dimension. I realized that I could make people *feel* things—happiness, sadness, or suspense—when they read my words. I liked that idea. After that, I wrote stories and poems whenever I could. Although it was sometimes embarrassing and scary, I began to let people read what I wrote more often. I dreamed about being a published writer, but it never occurred to me that it could happen before I "grew up."

Then, in seventh grade, a caring English teacher entered my poems in a national contest. I won! Two of my poems—one about a sunrise and another about flowers—were published in an anthology with other winning poems. How exciting to see the words I had carefully chosen and arranged *myself* transformed from scrawls on looseleaf paper to typeset words in a book. And there, under the title of each, was my name in boldface type. Suddenly, I felt different. I had always known that I was a writer, but now everyone would know—at least everyone who read the anthology. I was hooked on this business of publishing.

Many years and many bylines later, the thrill remains. I still feel a rush of excitement when I open an acceptance letter from a publisher. I still feel pride when I open a magazine and see my name in it. The writing process itself is satifying, but when something is published for others to read, the pleasure doubles.

Today my career is writing and editing. Those early publishing experiences were so encouraging that they led to my career choice. As an editor at the Children's Better Health Institute, I enjoy being able to publish many of today's children for the first time in our magazines.

We publish six children's magazines, and each of them features different kinds of reader participation. We receive hundreds of stories, letters, and poems, and thousands of drawings each month. Only a small number of these are published, however. We don't have enough room to publish them all. Instead, we look at every submission and try to choose the ones that we think are best. It's a hard job! To make it easier, we ask ourselves these four questions each time we evaluate a reader's submission:

1. *Is the story or poem original?* By original, we mean that it must be material that the child has written all by him or herself. Sometimes children copy a favorite poem or story from a book and claim that it is theirs. This is called plagiarism, and it's illegal. We try never to publish material copied from another source.

2. *How creative is the story or poem?* Sometimes children write what they think we editors want to see. Sometimes they write stories or poems that are too much like stories or poems they've already read in our magazines. But we look for different ideas. A fresh theme or an unusual subject—even an ordinary subject treated in an unusual way—shows creativity. We want to encourage our readers to be creative and use their imaginations as much as possible.

3. *Is the story or poem the right length for our magazines?* Because our pages are few and our page size small, our space is limited. We cannot use stories that require more than two magazine pages, or poems that take up more than one-fourth of our poetry-page. This means that we must sometimes refuse stories that are very good just because they are too long. This happens to professional writers sometimes, too. Learning to follow editorial guidelines is part of learning to become a published writer.

4. *Is the submission neat?* At CBHI, we don't expect a reader's submission to be typed (although it is nicer when they are). We do expect a story or poem to be written in legible handwriting or neat printing, preferably in ink. We like the stories or poems to be as error-free as possible, but we know that everyone makes spelling or punctuation mistakes sometimes. We just want to see evidence that the writer did his or her very best work. Sometimes it's helpful to have a teacher or parent read a story before it's sent. A grown-up can help look up correct spellings and usage in a dictionary. (A dictionary can be a writer's best friend!)

By keeping these tips in mind, you may increase your chances of having a story or poem published in a CBHI magazine. But if you get a letter from us saying, "Sorry, your material wasn't chosen," don't get discouraged. Instead, take another look at your submission. Are there ways you can improve it? Review the questions above. If you can answer yes to all of them, then your story or poem is probably your best effort. Try us again with something else. The more you write, the easier and more fun it will become. Sooner or later, you're sure to see your byline on a printed page, if you keep at it.

Russell Bennett
Editor-in-chief of Raintree Publishers

Russell Bennett, editor-in-chief at Raintree Publishers, says that, "At the risk of sounding corny: in all my years in publishing, the Publish-A-Book Contest at Raintree has been the most gratifying project I've ever worked on."

Raintree Publishers has sponsored the Publish-A-Book Contest annually for the past four years. Fourth, fifth, and sixth-grade students from all over the United States and Canada have submitted more than 25,000 stories in that time. We have awarded over $10,000 in prizes to the winners and their sponsors.

As a leading publisher of books for children and instructional support materials, Raintree began the contest with the idea of, "Let's do something for the kids!" Reading and writing go hand-in-hand, and we saw a creative writing contest as a way to promote reading. What better inspiration than the prospect of publication!

Each year, Raintree has published the first-place winner's story in addition to awarding a cash prize of $500 and ten free copies of his or her professionally illustrated, hard-cover book. Twenty second-place winners each receive a certificate and a $25 cash prize. The teachers or librarians who sponsor the winners receive free books from Raintree's catalog.

Due to the tremendous support and participation that has been shown over the years, Raintree decided to expand the awards. The 1988 Contest will have four Grand Prize Winners. Their stories will be published in the fall of that year, each student receiving free copies of the book and $500 cash. Twenty students will receive honorable mention; a certificate, and $25 cash. We'll also encourage the submission of color illustrations with the manuscripts.

Sheila Cowing
Editor of Shoe Tree, *published by the National Association for Young Writers*

Sheila Cowing, the current editor of Shoe Tree *and the* NAYW News, *has received considerable recognition for her writing. She is the recipient of the New Jersey State Distinguished Artist Fellowship Award for poetry (1987). And her book,* Our Wild Wetlands, *was named one of 1981's "outstanding science books for children" by the Children's Book Council and Science Teachers of America. Her poetry, articles, and literary criticism have appeared in several literary journals.*

She enjoys being the new editor of Shoe Tree *because she wants to encourage young writers. Here, she writes about her own first attempts at writing, and shares tips for submitting work to* Shoe Tree.

As a child, I was a closet writer. I started to write at four, and was, frankly, laughed at. In school, my stories and poems were praised, but I needed rave notices, and there were none. Still, writing was my way out of the dark, so I wrote, sometimes only in journals.

I planned journalism as a career, but in college I became anxious about the competition, so backed into my closet where I wrote only in notebooks for a number of years. Coming out was like a religious conversion.

As the editor of a children's magazine, I am now in a position where I can encourage other aspiring writers.

Shoe Tree is a literary magazine for writers ages six to fourteen. It comes out three times during the school year. At *Shoe Tree*, we care passionately about good writing. We publish the finest stories, poems, and non-fiction personal narratives that students can write. We publish work young writers are proud of.

Writers may submit at any time, year-round. When you send us work, tell us if the work is fiction or non-fiction. The writing must be your own work and should be neatly written or typed. Be sure to include your name, address, age, and the name of your school and teacher. Your story may be as long as you want. If we can't publish it all in one issue, we'll print it in installments. We also welcome foreign language submissions if they are accompanied by an English translation. If you would like your submission returned, please enclose a stamped, self-addressed envelope. Sending an SASE is customary whenever you write to a publication, even for information or submission guidelines.

Each spring, *Shoe Tree* sponsors a contest. In past years we have received as many as three thousand entries from all over the country. This year, we will again award prizes in three categories: fiction, nonfiction, and poetry. The 1988 contest will be our fourth and last annual competition. Beginning fall 1988, *Shoe Tree* will offer a different contest for each issue. Write to us for guidelines or see our contest listing on page 143.

Over the years we have published some wonderful stories, personal narratives, and poems. The best are always written from the heart. I believe that is where all fine art originates, in deep, human caring. Draw from your own feelings and experience.

After they are written, the best literary pieces are reworked. Writing is joyous and absorbing when that surge of words rolls out. The writer is proud and elated. Two hours or days later, he or she looks hard at his work with an objective eye. It is part of the process of caring for one's writing. He/she will want to remove words or put words in, changing phrases. The whole piece may have to be rewritten. It is hard work. It is what creates clean, beautiful writing.

As a writer, you will observe everything, everywhere you go, with all your senses. You'll notice the smell of morning, the color of the bus driver's jacket, how your notebook feels to your fingers as you carry it. As a writer, you'll use these details; your stories and poems will be rich with them. You cannot hold your readers unless they can imagine the experience, and they do that following your detailed direction. Notice details when you read, too. Literature is full of them.

Writing is an art. It's hard to do well, and a lot of people are trying and submitting work. Fortunately, there is no one right way, and no single editor can decide once and for all what is fine art. Keep at it. Because there is only one of you in all time; your expression is unique. You may not be able to decide how good that expression is or how it compares with others. You can only keep yourself open to experience and keep writing.

Marcia Preston
Editor of Byline, *sponsor of student writing contests*

Besides being a publisher/editor and former English teacher, Marcia Preston continues to write, as she's done for the past twenty years, and submit material to other editors. Her favorite genre is the short story, many of which she has sold to Woman's World, Teen, *the confession market and a literary magazine. She says she also likes to write nonfiction — because it's so much easier to sell — and poetry, though she doesn't consider herself an accomplished poet. She's written two novels, both as yet unpublished, and in her words, "has begun 'barely' a third."*

When not working as a writer and publisher, Ms. Preston and her husband enjoy working in their large gardens, one of which has a gazebo and water lily pond they built themselves.

Encouraging young writers is high on Ms. Preston's priority list. Here, she shares how Byline's *Student Contests were born and tips for entering and winning them.*

When I took over *Byline* magazine in March 1986, one of the first things my managing editor, Kathryn Fanning, and I discussed was the addition of a special feature for young writers. I'd been an English teacher for thirteen years, and most of those years I taught creative writing. The creative energies of young people are exciting and remarkable. My students never ceased to amaze and delight me with their wacky, original ideas. Kathryn and I both wanted to offer students an incentive to improve their writing.

Our Student Page gives young writers a chance to write for deadlines on specific topics through our contests. But best of all it offers a chance for publication. We publish our Student Page (which is actually two pages each issue) from September through May to coincide with the school year. In 1987 we began offering one contest per month, with cash prizes and publication for the winning entries. We also plan to add a column containing tips for young writers. These tips may be how-to items on improving writing, or information on other contests, or writing opportunities for students.

We also offer a wide selection of contests for adult writers, and many students want to enter those. We advise them to enter the student contest instead, because they obviously have a better chance of winning there. Besides, we seldom publish winners of the adult contests, but we do publish our student winners. Still, some high school writers feel ready to enter the adult categories, and there's certainly no rule against that. For younger writers, it's more realistic to stick with the contest designed especially for students.

The students who win our contests and get published on our pages seem to have a few things in common. They plan ahead. We list our contests several months in advance. Students can look ahead and plan for the ones they want to enter, then have plenty of time to do their best work. Our winners show a lot of creativity, but they also show a disciplined approach to their writing. We can tell they have checked their work carefully for correct spelling and grammar, and I'll bet the winning entries are not first drafts, either. Any professional writer can attest to the importance of reconsidering and rewriting to achieve the best manuscript he can possibly produce.

Professional writers have to work against deadlines, and this is another way entering contests can help a young writer toward professional quality in his work.

We have two requirements that might discourage some students, but we hope not. Those requirements are a small entry fee and a teacher's signature on the first page of the manuscript. Those entry fees not only pay the contest prizes, but help with the expenses of printing the feature in our magazine. Typesetting and printing are very expensive. Our Student Page costs us money to produce, but we believe it's worth the expense. As for the teacher's signature, call me suspicious, but I taught school for a long time and many a young poet tried to get his grade with a poem that turned out to be the lyrics to a rock song he thought I wouldn't know. (And sometimes I didn't; but the other students did!) Would you want to compete in a contest against a professional song writer? If the teacher signs, at least we have one more opinion that the manuscript is original.

Here are some tips on winning and getting published at *Byline*. First, write a story or poem about something you really believe in. It will show. Second, follow the rules and submit the neatest, most correct manuscript you can. Third, even if you don't win, keep trying. Those two words are the key to anybody's success and should be engraved on the forehead of all aspiring young writers. Believe in yourself and KEEP TRYING.

Carla J. Crane
Editor of Straight

In 1987, Carla Crane became the new editor of Straight, *a Christian magazine for teens that also often buys material from teens. She brings to her post an understanding of what it's like to be a hopeful young teen writer. Before submitting to a religious-oriented market, young writers need to be aware of the subtle differences between the secular and religious markets. Here, Ms. Crane shares her early beginnings as a published writer and why she switched to writing religous-oriented material.*

I was a teenage columnist. Yes, at the age of fifteen I was chosen to be guest columnist in my hometown newspaper. I was selected from my journalism class to write a weekly column about life in high school. Not only did I get a byline, but my picture appeared each week as well. I thought I'd hit the big time!

From there I went on to news editor of my high school paper and staff reporter on my college newspaper. But it was during my first semester in college while reporting student council meetings that I began to question my future as a journalist. It seemed that all I was doing was listening to the petty arguments of the council officers. *Surely my writing is worth more than reporting the depressing and negative,* I thought. *Shouldn't writing encourage and uplift as well as report?*

So I transferred to a Bible college and majored in journalism. It was in that positive environment that I discovered writing can do more than simply report. Writing can encourage, uplift, and teach. And I discovered that writing for a Christian market was a good way to share my faith and encourage others.

While in Bible college, I began working on the school newspaper. My senior year I was selected as editor of our yearbook. And it was also in college that I wrote my first assignment for pay—a devotion to be used on the back of a church bulletin cover. Little did I know that the company that produced those bulletins, Standard Publishing, would later hire me. After working for three years as an assistant editor, I am now the editor of *Straight*, a magazine designed for teenagers.

If you're interested in writing for *Straight*, there are some things to keep in mind. *Straight* buys poems, short stories, and essays from teenagers thirteen to nineteen years old. Our audience is Christian teenagers in church Sunday schools. Personal experiences and insights are often accepted as long as they deal with the individual's faith. A birthdate is required with teen submissions, as well as a Social Security number (provided that you live in the United States and are not too young to have one).

There are a few things I would like to say to aspiring writers in general.

Learn to rewrite. The difference between a good writer and a great writer is one who can edit his own work. One of the hardest things to do as a writer is to look at your work objectively. I've had more experience as an editor than a writer. But to be good at either you must be able to do both. By editing your own work, you will only improve it. Learn to strive for excellence instead of average.

Know your audience. This is especially important when writing for the religious market. Don't write an inspirational piece in the same style you would write an English report.

Read. A good writer should also be a good reader. The best way to expand your vocabulary is by reading. The more you read, the more you'll learn.

Don't give up. If you're really serious about writing, strive to have your work published. And don't be discouraged when you receive a rejection letter. Most people will hear *no* before they hear *yes*.

When I became that young columnist at fifteen, I never imagined that I'd someday be the editor of a magazine for teenagers. I don't consider myself to be a great writer, but I do consider myself blessed. I'm blessed because I received opportunities early in life to discover and hone my talents. And I'm blessed because I'm in a position to help other young people find and develop theirs!

Linda Hutton
Editor of Rhyme Time Poetry
Newsletter

*Linda Hutton has been a prolific writer since
grade school. With the encouragement of high
school English teachers she turned out reams
of short stories, some of which were printed in
the school's literary publication. As an adult,
she wrote and edited several business publica-
tions before becoming a full-time freelance writer and the publisher/editor
of four publications:* Rhyme Time Poetry Newsletter *(bimonthly),* Writer's
Info *(monthly),* Mystery Time *(annually), and* Best of Rhyme Time *(annually). Aimed primarily at adults, all four publications are open to young writers
who believe in themselves and are willing to polish their work. She also is
responsible for market information for a number of other writer-oriented
publications.*

*She began selling her own work in 1977 and credits her continued success
by having over 500 manuscripts in circulation at any time. That's a lot of
writing!*

*Ms. Hutton says she never watches television — doesn't even own a set —
because she finds the plots insultingly thin and the story lines weak. Always
a voracious reader, her proudest possessions include the complete works of
Agatha Christie and those of Rex Stout. Ms. Hutton speaks often at writer's
conferences on several topics including marketing, mystery novel writing,
and poetry. "I feel qualified to give advice," she says, "having made every
possible mistake when I started out."*

Writing poetry can be the easiest thing you'll ever do, or it can be
as difficult as getting your father's Buick on Saturday night. I had
more success with poetry—I *never* had the family car to drive in high
school in Montana, but I did sell my poems.

Every library has books on how to write poetry, how to read it aloud
and how to study poetry. Check them out. When you find a poet whose
work you admire and understand, read it over and over so the rhythms
become natural to you. Learn how that poet arranges words and what
they mean; do they paint word pictures? Now try to write a poem of

your own using that same style. We all have to imitate someone's style when we start out; later you can develop your own style and then others will imitate you.

Carry a notepad with you and write down thoughts that come to you, or good descriptions you read, or something you see happening at school. When you have a quiet moment, study your scribblings to find one that makes you think, or feel, or dream, then write a poem about it. At first, just try to write your feelings. Later you can try to write a haiku, or a quatrain, or even a sonnet. It's like borrowing that car again: First you ask if you can just drive to the library for a book on poetry and next time, drive across the state to go to a rock concert. You're not going to write a sonnet on your first try and you're certainly not going to hear the *Grateful Dead* the first time you ask.

The first poem you write is going to be lousy, so don't waste a good piece of paper on it. Use scratch paper. Maybe your second and third poems will be trashers, too, but eventually you'll turn out something good. You'll feel good about it and people who read your poem will understand your meaning. Now you're ready to send it off to a magazine or a contest. There's no point in being another Emily Dickinson, who hid her poems in a drawer for her sister to find after Emily died. I want cash while I'm still alive to spend it and I'm sure you do, too.

I hope you're taking typing (I flunked it), because you'll need to type your poem very carefully. Your poem must be centered on the page with lots of nice white space around it, and it must be typed double-spaced. When you have it typed perfectly, before you put your name on it, run half a dozen photocopies. Some contests don't allow your name to show anywhere on your entry, while others specify it must be in the left-hand corner or the right-hand corner or on the back. With all these photocopies, you can prepare your entry exactly as the rules decree and enter it in several contests at once if the rules allow.

Don't use a pen name and don't put *any* extra information on your poem. No one cares how you felt when you wrote it, or where you were or what the date was. The editor wants to see only your poem, presented in your best professional manner. You might have to give your birth date for contests restricted to young writers.

There, does that sound easy? Well, if it does, you haven't been paying attention. You not only won't sell your poem, you won't get the car this weekend, so walk back and read the instructions again.

CHAPTER FOUR

How to Prepare Your Manuscript

The best way to prepare a manuscript before submitting it to a market or contest is by following the same standard formats used by professional writers. That means resisting the urge to use scented or colored paper, fancy typewriter type, hand-drawn pictures in the margins, or special folders or covers for your material. Stick to an ordinary black ribbon and plain white paper that measures 8 1/2 x 11 inches. Using anything else will brand you as an amateur from the first whiff of lilacs to the last curlicue of your signature.

There's nothing wrong with being a young, inexperienced writer. But if you're serious about getting published, you don't want to *look* like a young, inexperienced writer.

Remember, editors haven't time to be entertained by the way manuscripts are prepared. They have barely enough time to read and select submissions. So, to give your writing the best possible chance of attracting an editor's eye, follow the formats outlined here. If you feel you need to overlook or bypass some of the rules, be very sure you have a sound reason for doing so. This is one time where it's best to follow the logical side of your mind and not the creative side.

Of course, for very young writers who will be handprinting their material, the guidelines are less strict. Still, if a young writer wishes to send along any artwork, it is best to use a separate sheet of paper rather than draw, paint, or color directly on the written manuscript.

Typewritten Material

Use non-erasable sixteen to twenty pound white bond paper. Never use erasable typing paper for a final manuscript. It smudges and smears too easily and may give an editor's sleeve an unwanted tie-dyed effect. For simple mistakes, use a light film of liquid correction fluid or the newer (and neater looking) liquid correction paper. If you need to correct or delete an entire sentence, try press-on correction tape available at office supply stores.

Always use a good, black typewriter ribbon which produces a clean, dark, easy-to-read type. Never use colored ribbon. Replace worn or faded ribbons before typing your final manuscript.

Use standard twelve-point pica or ten-point elite type. With the advent of the ball and daisy wheel, it's easy to get carried away with exotic typefaces and unusual size print. Resist the urge. Never use a fancy script typeface. Editors find it too much of a strain to read. Save it for personal correspondence.

Leave ample margins on all four sides of each sheet of paper. The standard rule is to leave at least a 1¼ inch margin on both the top and bottom of your page, plus a full inch on each side. This not only makes for a neater appearance but will give editors, and you, plenty of space to make corrections.

For *all* manuscripts, except poetry, double-space your lines. *This is one rule which should never be broken.* To double-space, set the line spacing lever on your typewriter to number two. This will leave a full line of empty space between each line of type.

For poetry, type your poem as you wish it to appear, double-spacing between verses if necessary. With the exception of your first page, plan on twenty-six lines of manuscript type on each page. If you find yourself always typing too close to the bottom of the page, try marking lightly with a pencil where your last line of type should be. Then erase the line later.

Typing the same number of lines on each page will make it easier to estimate the number of words in your finished manuscript. With proper margins and twenty-six lines of type, you will average two hundred and fifty words to a page.

You will use a slightly different format for the first page of your manuscript. (See figure 1 on page 50.) At the top of your first page, starting at the left margin, use single-spacing to type your name,

your name,
address, phone
Soc. Security
number here →

Susie Kaufmann
2151 Hale Rd.
Sandusky MI 48471
(313) 555-2076
SS#000-00-0000

About 800 words ← *word count*
      Oct. 29, 1985 ← *date*

THE STOLEN TEST ← *title*
by
Susie Kaufmann ← *author*

start your
story here → Karen Mathis hurried down the deserted hall of Mayville

Junior High. She was late. There would be no time to

study before supper now.

   "Darn," she grumbled. She was annoyed with herself

for leaving her history book in the gym. She had walked

nearly half way home before remembering it.

   The empty building echoed with an eerie, hollow sound

like a cave along the seashore. Somewhere, a janitor

whistled "Yankee Doodle" as he slushed a pail of water

down a drain.

   A door creaked behind her. Karen spun around. Her

armload of books slipped. She caught them before they

fell.

   "It's okay, Bud," someone whispered. "It's just

Karen."

   Travis Piper and Bud Watson slipped quietly out of

Figure 1.

address, and telephone number with the area code. Then type your
Social Security number. If you don't have a Social Security number,
include your date of birth. Editors must have this information in their
files before paying writers for material.

At the top right-hand margin, across from your name, type the
approximate number of words contained in your manuscript. (I also
like to include the date I mailed my manuscript. You can easily add

this later just before mailing by printing it neatly with a black pen.)

Drop about one-third of the way down the page and using capital letters, type the title of your manuscript. Under the title, center the word "by," then center your name the way you wish it to read in print.

Switch your typewriter to double-space, drop down two lines and begin your story or article. Remember to leave the one-inch margin at the bottom.

Editors will use the empty space that you have left on the top of your first page to write notes to the typesetter or copyeditor.

If you wish to include a title page, type it exactly as you would the first page of your manuscript without including any of the story. It is not necessary to include a title page with a manuscript that is less than six to eight pages long.

last name →

key word from title ↓

page number ↓

Kaufmann   STOLEN TEST   2

Mrs. Taylor's history room. "Let's get out of here,"

Travis whispered. He grabbed Karen by the arm and rushed

her toward the door.

"Wait a minute," Karen objected. "What's going on?"

"Shut-up," Travis ordered. "We'll fill you in outside."

The three hurried out of the building. The sun was

beginning to settle behind the closely knit suburban homes.

Travis's firm grip of Karen's arm hurt. She struggled

to break loose.

Figure 2.

For the second page and each page after, type your last name in the upper left-hand corner, center a key word or phrase from your title on the same line, and put the page number on the right. (See figure 2 on page 51.) This will help an editor put your story back in order if it should get dropped or shuffled around.

At the end of your manuscript, drop down two lines and center the words "The End." This may seem a little silly but a busy editor or typesetter will appreciate knowing for certain when he's come to the end of your piece. Journalists center the number thirty (–30–) instead of typing "The End." You may use this, too.

Never staple or bind your manuscript together in any way.

If you wish to tell the editor something about yourself or give some added information about your story or article such as how you came to write it, you may do so on a separate sheet of paper called a "cover letter." This letter is written like a regular personal or business letter with your name, address, telephone number, and date at the top plus the name and address of the publication to whom you are writing. If possible, locate the name of the editor in a current issue of that publication. Then begin the letter, Dear Mr. or Ms. with the editor's last name. If you don't have the editor's name, simply write Dear Editor.

Make your cover letter as short as possible, never more than one page. Tell the editor only those things which relate directly to the manuscript you are sending. Though editors may be interested in knowing all about you, your family, your friends, and your hobbies, they probably do not have time to read about you now. If editors want more information, they will ask you to send another letter. Remember you are trying to interest the editor in your manuscript, not in you personally.

If your manuscript is four pages or less, fold it carefully in thirds. It will then fit neatly into a number ten business size envelope. (Do not use a smaller envelope. Manuscripts are almost impossible to read or correct when all creased up.) Also include another envelope of the same size addressed to yourself. Attach the same amount of postage on this *inside* envelope that you will need on the outside envelope. This extra envelope is known as a SASE—self-addressed stamped envelope. *You must include a SASE (self-addressed stamped envelope) any time you write to any editor or contest for information or when you submit a manuscript for consideration.* The editor will use this envelope to return your manuscript to you if he decides not to accept it, or to send the material you have requested.

If your manuscript is more than four pages long or if you are including artwork or photographs, use a large manila envelope which will hold your material without having to fold it.

When addressing your mailing envelope, use the editor's name whenever possible. Such as:

> Thumbprints
> Joan Sayers, Editor
> 215 Ellington Street
> Caro, MI 48723

You can locate the name of the current editor by checking the masthead, usually located near the front of the publication.

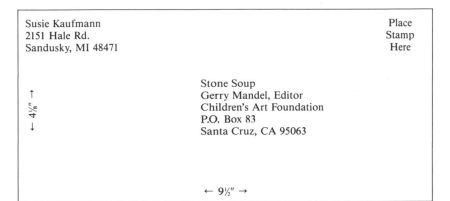

Figure 3. Sample Mailing Envelope

Stone Soup
P.O. Box 83
Santa Cruz, CA 95063

Place
Stamp
Here

↑
4⅛″
↓

Susie Kaufmann
2151 Hale Rd.
Sandusky, MI 48471

← 9½″ →

Figure 4. Sample SASE

Protect artwork or photographs by placing them between pieces of cardboard. *Never* use a staple or paper clip on a photo. It will ruin it. *Never* write on the back of a photo with a pen or a pencil. Put the information on an address label which can be stuck to the back of the photo. You can also write safely on the back of a photo using a special grease pencil found in art and office supply stores.

Use a second manila envelope for your self-addressed stamped envelope (SASE.) Fold it in half to fit in the mailing envelope. Remember to include enough postage to have your material mailed back to you.

An editor will not return your material if you forget to enclose a self-addressed stamped envelope with the right amount of postage. Some editors will not even read a manuscript that is not accompanied by a SASE. This may not seem like a good way to do business, but editors cannot afford to pay for the return of manuscripts from every writer who submits material. It would cost them thousands of dollars each year! They would rather use the money to pay writers for work that is accepted for publication.

A few of the markets listed state they do not return material at all. You do not need to include a self-addressed stamped envelope with

Place
Stamp
Here

←3½″→

YOUR NAME
YOUR ADDRESS
CITY, STATE, ZIP CODE

← 5½″ →

Figure 5. Front of postcard

TITLE OF YOUR STORY _____

DATE YOU MAILED IT _____

(WHO YOU MAILED IT TO)

_____

_____
Received by

_____
Date

Figure 6. Message side of postcard

your material when submitting manuscripts to these markets and contests.

If you are worried that your package may not reach an editor, or if you want to make sure your manuscript did arrive at a market which will not send it back, you may enclose a special self-addressed stamped postcard. (See figures 5 and 6.) Most editors will take the time to mark a postcard and return it to you.

Always make a copy of your manuscript when submitting to a market that will return your work, and *especially* to those that won't. It is insurance against a manuscript that is damaged or gets lost in the mail. Occasionally, an editor will want to discuss your manuscript with you over the phone. It is much easier when you both have a copy to look at.

Copies can be made using carbon paper, retyping a piece, using a photocopying machine, or storing a copy on a computer disk.

Handwritten Material

If at all possible, type your manuscript or have someone type it for you. However, some editors who are willing to receive material from young people thirteen and under do not mind receiving handwritten or handprinted material as long as it is neat and legible.

Unless you have excellent cursive handwriting, print your manuscript. Check editors' guidelines for their preference.

Use separate sheets of white-lined, loose-leaf paper for handwritten manuscripts. Wide-ruled paper is best if you tend to write big. If you use narrow-ruled paper, be sure to write on *every other line.* It will make it much easier for an editor to read.

Follow the same rules of format for preparing each page of your manuscript that apply to typewritten material.

Write on *only one side of the paper.* Remember to number each sheet.

Never use paper torn from a notebook. The pages tend to stick together and bits of the edges are always falling off, making a mess.

For very young writers, it is okay to use tablet paper with ruled lines. Remember to write on only one side of the sheet. Put the pages in order but leave them loose. Never bind or staple them together. (If a teacher is submitting several copies of her students' work, a paper clip may be used on each individual manuscript.)

Make corrections on handwritten material by drawing a line neatly through the mistake, then going on. If you make a lot of mistakes on one page, rewrite the whole page.

Use the same guidelines for mailing handwritten manuscripts as with typewritten material. Follow the market tip sheet for submitting art or photographs.

Computer Printouts

As personal computers and word processors become more popular, editors are agreeing to read manuscripts done on a computer if a letter-quality or laser printer is used. Most dot-matrix printing is too light in color and hard to read. If you use tractor-fed paper be sure the finished size measures 8½ x 11 inches instead of larger size computer paper.

Follow the same guidelines as those for preparing and mailing the typewritten manuscript. Be sure to number and separate the printout sheets before mailing.

Plays and Scripts

The standard format for preparing scripts for radio and theatre differs from the written formats for stories, poems, articles, and fillers. It would be best to check with your librarian or teacher for help in locating a sample script. Study it carefully. Notice the differences in typing dialogue, description, and sound effects. Use the sample script as a reference when you type your play or radio script.

Sample scripts may also be found in many language arts books. If you need more help, check with the drama teacher at your school, or ask for advice from someone involved with your community theatre.

When submitting a play or script to a magazine leave the pages unbound. However, most theatre groups and contests prefer scripts which are submitted in light-weight folders or grip binders.

Exceptions to the Rule

There may be times when you want to send an editor material prepared in a special way. Just remember to include the *written part* of the manuscript on a separate sheet of paper following the standard formats as best you can. Then if the editor decides to publish your material, he will be able to give this copy to the typesetter to use.

Here are some examples where you might consider breaking the standard formats for submitting material:

SITUATION: You do beautiful calligraphy work and your manuscript tells teens how you make extra money by designing and selling personalized stationary.

YOU MIGHT: Prepare your manuscript following the standard formats. Then include as your cover letter a short message written on a sheet of stationary that you have designed.

SITUATION: Your class has put together a special collection of stories written and illustrated by the students. One of the students, or your teacher, has written an article about the project.

YOU MIGHT: Type the article using the standard formats plus include a free copy of your book for the editor to read.

SITUATION: You have a handicap that makes it difficult to type or write neatly.

YOU MIGHT: Prepare your manuscript the best you can. Include a cover letter telling a bit about yourself. Consider having someone else help you prepare your final copy.

SITUATION: For a Christmas present, you typed some of your poems on special paper, then illustrated or decorated them yourself and hung them in pretty frames.

YOU MIGHT: Retype your poem on a separate sheet of paper using the standard format. Include this with a photograph of your framed poem, or include an extra illustrated poem for the editor.

Keeping Track of Submissions

Once you decide to submit material to an editor or contest, you must also devise a system of keeping track of your manuscripts. This is especially important if you are anxious to get published and will be sending more than one manuscript out at the same time.

One way to keep track is with three-by-five index cards kept in a file box. Prepare a new index card for each manuscript you send out. Along the top of each card write these headings:

	DATE	DATE
TITLE	MAILED	RETURNED
MARKET		NOTES

↑
3″
↓

← 5″ →

Figure 7.

Record the title of your manuscript or contest entry, the date you mailed it (not the date you wrote it), and the name of the market or contest where you sent the manuscript. Under "Notes" you may want to write down the amount of postage it cost to mail the manuscript. Include the cost of the self-addressed stamped envelope and/or postcard too.

When you receive an answer from the editor or contest, write the date under the "Date Returned" heading. Under "Notes" or on the back of the card, mark whether the manuscript was accepted or rejected and any other information such as how much you were (or will be) paid for the piece, and/or when the editor plans to publish it.

If the manuscript was rejected, select another market from the list. Mark the new information on the same card if there is room.

If students will be submitting material as part of a class project, one file box may be used to keep an accurate record of all student submissions and editors' remarks.

Similar records may also be kept in an extra notebook.

Additional Tips

Think ahead! If you're really anxious to submit material, don't wait until you have a manuscript in final draft form before sending away for market guidelines, sample copies, and detailed contest information. But don't send away for all of them at once either. Choose a few markets and contests that are looking for material similar to what you are most interested in writing. Consider also markets and contests directed especially toward young people your age.

Once the market and contest information begins arriving, you'll want an easy way to store it, so when you have a manuscript ready to submit, you can consult your market information and choose where you would like to send it first.

All this information can be kept in a desk drawer, file cabinet, or even a shoe box. An even better method is to make your own personal marketing guide. You'll need a large three ring binder and a box of vinyl sheet protectors. Top-loading sheet protectors work best. You might also want a package of tab dividers to separate various types of markets and contests, or to file information alphabetically.

When a sample copy and guideline sheet arrive, slip them into a sheet protector for safe keeping. Some sample copies won't fit into the sheet protector. You'll have to store these somewhere else. Put a note on the corresponding guideline sheet to remind yourself where the sample copy is. Insert a reference sheet at the front of your binder to record which market and contest information you have. Also include the date you received the information and the date of the sample copy so you'll know when you need to send for more current information.

Your personal marketing guide is also an excellent place to keep additional notes about writing, the names and addresses of new markets and contests, and even your record of submissions. If you attend young author conferences, writing workshops, or have published authors speak to your class, store your notes or any handout material in your marketing guide for easy reference.

CHAPTER FIVE

Understanding a Market Listing

Markets, which include secular and religious magazines, newspapers, newsletters, and book publishers, are arranged alphabetically for easy reference.

Each listing contains three individual sections of information which will help you understand (1) the type of publication it is, (2) what material it will consider from young people, and (3) how to submit your work. There are two optional sections. "Editor's Remarks" are quotes directly from editors or their guideline sheets. They provide additional information to help you submit your material to the appropriate publication. The "Subscription Rates" section has been included as an extra service since so many of the publications listed are available by subscription only.

There are thirty-seven new market and contest listings in this edition of *Market Guide for Young Writers*, marked with a dagger (†) so they can be easily located.

Markets which are especially eager to receive manuscripts from young people are preceded with an asterisk (*). Markets which require a prepaid fee are marked with a dollar sign ($).

Information for each listing was provided directly from the publication through our survey and is as current as possible.

The following chart and sample market listing will help explain the information contained within each section.

MARKET LISTING CHART

SECTION	YOU WILL FIND	PAY SPECIAL ATTENTION TO
1	Name of Publication. Mailing address for manuscripts, guidelines, and sample copies. Brief description including how often it is published, the age and interests of its readers.	Who reads this publication and the general theme followed in each issue.
2	Types of written material, art, and photographs which are considered for publication Specific material which is not accepted.	Any special columns or departments written exclusively by young writers. Any specific types of material which are never used.
3	More detailed information to help you write and prepare your manuscripts. Payments offered; rights purchased. Word limits; line limits for poetry. Availability of guidelines and samples.	Any special instructions for submitting manuscripts. Whether you need to include a signed statement from your parent or teacher or guardian.
4	Advice and helpful tips especially for young writers quoted directly from the editor.	What the editors say they do and do not want from young writers.
5	Subscription rates. Subscription mailing address when it differs from the editorial office.	Included as an extra service for young writers, parents, and teachers.

SAMPLE MARKET LISTING

1 ————**LISTEN, JOURNAL OF BETTER LIVING,** 6830 Laurel Street NW, Washington DC 20012. A monthly publication for teens and young adults encouraging the development of good habits and high ideals of physical and mental health.

2 ————**Publishes:** Special column for teens called "Graffiti" which uses short, well-written, thought-provoking poems, stories, and essays from teen writers. Also uses factual features or opinion essays with or without accompanying quality photos, narratives based on true-life incidents, poetry, puzzles, and cartoons.

3 ————**Submission Info:** Submissions for "Graffiti" should include age, grade, school, etc., no photos. Poetry should not be longer than 20 lines; stories and essays 300–500 words. Address to "Graffiti" in care of *Listen* magazine. Include SASE. Send for free writer's guidelines and tip sheet. Samples available for $1 and large manila envelope with SASE. Pays $10 for poems; $15–$20 for stories and essays. Varying rates for other material.

4 ————**Editor's Remarks:** "*Listen* is circulated in public high schools and junior high schools, so religious material is not suitable."

5 ————**Subscription Rates:** One year (12 issues) $11.95. Higher outside U.S. Send check or money order to *Listen,* P.O. Box 7000, Boise, ID 83707. Also available in many school libraries.

CHAPTER SIX

The Market List

On the following pages you will find the special market and contest lists for young writers. Yet, many of the best and most easily accessible markets are not listed here. They are the publications you are already familiar with, such as your hometown newspaper or the regional magazine insert that comes with the daily paper, your own school or church publication, and the special publications sponsored by clubs and organizations. These are all potential markets for your work. You may submit material to them using the same formats and advice you have learned about here.

Be sure to include a short cover letter when you first submit to these local markets. Tell the editor where you are from and include a bit of personal history such as the school you attend, your age and background about the manuscript you are sending. If the local editor likes your work, you may find yourself being asked to do special writing assignments.

†*$ AGORA: THE MAGAZINE FOR GIFTED STUDENTS, AG Publications, P.O. Box 10975, Raleigh, NC 27605. Sally R. Humble, Ph.D., Executive Editor. For gifted secondary school students and their teachers with English emphasis but interdisciplinary approach.

Publishes: Short stories and poems. Also essays with an interdisciplinary approach. Winners in writing competitions are eligible for printing. (*Author's note:* Be sure submission of a contest winning entry meets with contest requirements first.)

Submission Info: Writers in grades 7–12 and college preferred. Limit length of stories and essays to 4,000 words. Items of 500; 1,000; 1,500; and 2,000 words preferred. All submissions printed are copyrighted by magazine but author also retains rights. No payment for submissions at this time. Participants must subscribe or attend a school subscribing to a class set.

Subscription Rates: Individual subscription (4 issues during school year) $9. Class set (20 or more to one address) $7.50. Teacher's supplement $20.

†*$ THE APPLE BLOSSOM CONNECTION, P.O. Box 325, Stacyville, IA 50476. Monthly publication for writers of all ages.

Publishes: Open to all types of manuscripts: poetry, non-fiction, fiction on general topics as well as those specifically geared toward writers and the writing profession.

Subscription Info: Open to manuscripts from all age groups. Use standard formats. Include a short 50–100 word autobiographical sketch with first submission. (This is not mandatory but editors like to tell readers a little something about the writers who contribute.) Poetry: 36 line maximum. Non-fiction: 200–500 words. Fiction: 1,200 words maximum. Cartoons and illustrations are considered but must be done in black ink on white. No pencil sketches. Payment varies: 3–5 contributor copies; $5–$85; subscriptions, etc. Be sure to include SASE. Mail submissions to: J.D. Scheneman, Editor.

Editor's Remarks: "Revise and re-write your work before submitting it. Don't leave spelling errors, etc., for us to correct."

AVON BOOKS, 1790 Broadway, New York, NY 10019.

Publishes: Various book manuscripts for young readers. Avon Camelot is for readers 6–12. Not currently interested in picture books, poetry, fairy tales, animal stories, computer mysteries, historical novel, heavy problem novels, or non-fiction. Are considering fantasy, science fiction, mysteries (though very selective with mysteries), and contemporary and realistic novels with strong characters who may have problems but who make readers smile. Avon Flare is for readers 12–18. Young adult contemporary problem novels—but with a "light touch"—are preferred. Not currently interested in poetry, science fiction, or non-fiction for this age group. Very selective with fantasy, mystery, adventure, and romance. Send SASE for guidelines. (*Author's note:* This is the same information given to adult writers. The market is very tough.) Be sure to include adequate SASE for return of book-length manuscript. See guidelines for specifics on page length and other submission information.

Subscription Rates: One year $10. Two years $18.

BITTERROOT POETRY MAGAZINE, P.O.Box 489, Spring Glen, NY 12483–0489. An international poetry magazine appearing three times a year.

Publishes: "Good poetry." Submit 3–4 poems with #10 SASE. Payment, 1 copy. Rights revert to author after publication. Send unpublished poems only. Artwork accepted if in black and white or line drawings. Payment, 1 copy.

Submission Info: Address poems to Menke Katz, Editor; artwork to Rivke Katz.

Editor's Remarks: "It's best to see our magazine to know what we use. Poems are considered better if the *how* is stressed rather than *what* is said. Avoid wordiness, cliches, try to be as original as possible. Avoid over-used rhymes, or use no rhyme."

Subscription Rates: One year (3 issues) $10. Two years $18. Three years $25. Sample issue $3.75.

THE BLACK COLLEGIAN, 1240 South Broad St., New Orleans, LA 70125. Published four times a year for Black college seniors, grad students and young professionals.

Publishes: Non-fiction in six main areas: Job Hunting Tips, Overviews of Career Opportunities, Sources of Financial Aid and Other Forms of Assistance, Self-development Tips (such as how to cope with stress, time management, dressing your best on a tight budget, etc.), Analysis or Investigations of Conditions and Problems that affect

Blacks, and Celebrations of Black Success (such as interviews with and profiles of Black celebrities, role models and leaders, Black history, Black art and culture, etc. . . .) Also accepts photos and illustrations.

Submission Info: Prefers queries first but will review unsolicited manuscripts. Reports within a three week period. Editorial closing date for any given issue is always two months prior to publication date: e.g., July 1 for September issue. Normal payment range is $25 to $350. Usually buys one-time rights. Photographs accompanying articles should have legibly typed or written captions attached to the back of the prints, along with any desired photo credits. Pays $35 for black and white photos, $50 for color. Illustrations can be any medium, black and white or color. Any style from super-real to surreal. Any size. Send SASE for contributor's guidelines. Sample copy for 9 x 12 SAE and 3 first class stamps.

Editor's Remarks: "The word 'Black,' when used to refer to African, Africa-American or African-Diasporan people should be capitalized in all manuscripts sent in for review."

Subscription Rates: Available mainly at placement offices of over 1100 four-year colleges and universities. One year $10. Write to above address, Circulation Department.

†*$ BOY'S LIFE, 1325 Walnut Hill Lane, Irving, TX 75038–3096. Published by Boy Scouts of America.

Publishes: Exciting, funny or interesting first person adventure accounts from those under 18 for "Reader's Page." Does not publish poetry or puzzles from readers.

Submission Info: Address submissions to the attention of the Reader's Page Editor. Use standard formats. Prints only black and white photos. Does not pay for nor acknowledge contributions. No SASE needed. Writer's guidelines and sample copies are not available.

Subscription Rates: For registration and subscriptions write above address. Enclose check for $13.20 for one year subscription, $24.20 for two years. Special rates to Cub Scouts and Boy Scouts available through local council offices.

*BREAD MAGAZINE, 6401 The Paseo, Kansas City, MO 64131. Feature magazine for junior and senior high school students. Published monthly by the Church of the Nazarene.

Publishes: Articles which speak to junior and senior high youth in light of their spiritual pilgrimage and their pressing spiritual needs. Prefers articles written in first person. Occasionally uses fiction. Especially interested in material which follows these sample themes: talents, mysteries of Christianity, discipline, friendship and dating, family relationships, politics and the Christian, Christ's second coming, dealing with authority, discipleship, stewardship, back to school. Also uses some photos.

Submission Info: Payment for accepted freelance articles is 3 1/2¢ per word. Free sample and writer's guidelines available for SASE.

Editor's Remarks: "The periodical purports to: inspire faith in Jesus Christ, teach the fullness of the Holy Spirit, model personal growth and development, share life in the Body of Christ, the Church, encourage response to the Word of God, pioneer a personal devotional life, model relationships with family members, challenge love for others, impress ethical behavior, confront responsibility to the world."

Subscription Rates: One year $6.

* CHILD LIFE, 1100 Waterway Blvd., P.O. Box 567, Indianapolis, IN 46206. Monthly publication for children ages 7 to 9 from the Children's Better Health Institute. Stresses health-related themes or ideas including nutrition, safety, exercise, or proper health habits.

Publishes: From readers: fiction stories, poems, and occasionally puzzles, recipes and artwork.

Submission Info: Prefers stories and poems that are typed with double-spacing but will also accept contributions that are written legibly in ink. Put your name, age, school, and complete address on each page of your work. Fiction stories may be up to 500 words. Include SASE if you wish material to be returned if not accepted. No payment is made for published reader material. All contributors may purchase copies in which their work appears at a reduced rate. Send SASE for guidelines. Sample copies available for 75¢ each. Submissions should be limited to young people ages 7–9.

Editor's Remarks: "Unfortunately, because of the many thousands of contributions we receive, we are not able to publish everything sent in to us."

Subscription Rates: One year $11.95. Special rate of $9.97 is usually offered in every issue.

* CHILDREN'S DIGEST, 1100 Waterway Blvd, P.O. Box 567, Indianapolis, IN 46206. Monthly publication for children ages 8 to 10 from the Children's Better Health Institute. Stresses health-related themes or ideas including nutrition, safety, exercise and proper health habits.

Publishes: From readers: original fiction or non-fiction stories, original poetry, readers' favorite jokes and riddles, and readers' opinions on specific questions. All material should be health-related. This includes good nutrition, safety, exercise, or proper health habits. Also likes seasonal material.

Submission Info: Prefers stories and poems that are typed with double-spacing but will also accept contributions that are written legibly in ink. Put your name, age, school, and complete address on each page of your work. A personal photo and autobiography *do not need* to be include. Fiction and non-fiction stories may be up to 700 words in length. Include SASE if you wish material to be returned if not accepted. No payment is made for published reader material, but writers of "Young Author Stories" receive 2 complimentary copies of the issue in which their story appears. All contributors may purchase copies in which their work appears at a reduced rate. Send SASE for special guidelines for young writers. Sample copies available for 75¢ each.

Editor's Remarks: "We also like mysteries and humorous stories. Any seasonal material should be submitted eight months prior to publication. We usually select material sent in by children in the 8 to 12 age group. If you're older than 12, it would be best to find another market for your work. We feel that it is unfair for us to judge the work of young children against the work of teenagers."

Subscription Rates: One year $11.95. Special rate of $9.97 is usually offered in every issue.

†* **CHILDREN'S MAGIC WINDOW**, 6125 Olson Memorial, Minneapolis, MN 55422. Monthly mass-market children's magazine for ages 6–12.

Publishes: From young writers: letters, poems, drawing and stories for special "Kidstuff" pages. May also consider stories, poetry, features and information for columns for other areas of magazine.

Submission Info: Use standard format with 60-character line. Send SASE for guidelines. Sample copy available for $2.50. All manuscripts, queries, and editorial correspondence should be addressed to editor-in-charge, Mary Morse.

Subscription Rates: One year $16.98. Two years $29.98.

* **CHILDREN'S PLAYMATE**, 1100 Waterway Blvd., P.O. Box 567, Indianapolis, IN 46206. Monthly publication for children 5 to 7 from the Children's Better Health Institute. Stresses health-related themes or ideas including nutrition, safety, exercise, or proper health habits.

Publishes: From readers, original poems, original artwork, and jokes and riddles. Does not publish stories written by readers.

Submission Info: Poetry must have been made up by the reader himself. Artwork must be pictures drawn by the reader. Jokes and riddles can be favorite ones readers have heard. Poetry may or may not rhyme. Include SASE is you wish material to be returned if not accepted. No payment is made for published reader material. All contributors may purchase copies in which their work appears at a reduced rate. Send SASE for guidelines. Sample copies available for 75¢. Submissions should be limited to young people ages 5–7.

Editor's Remarks: "Unfortunately, because of the many thousands of contributions we receive, we are not able to publish everything sent in to us."

Subscription Rates: One year $11.95. Special rate of $9.97 is usually offered in every issue.

†* **CLUBHOUSE**, P.O. Box 15, Berrien Springs, MI 49103. Christian magazine for ages 9–14 by Your Story Hour.

Publishes: Short stories, poems, puzzles, crafts and recipes. Also special "Whooo Knows?" column which features questions and answers by subscribers. Because some church demoninations use *Clubhouse* as supplementary material, the magazine *cannot* accept material dealing with certain topics including: Santa Claus, elves, reindeer, etc.; Halloween, witches, ghosts, magic, etc.; space fantasy, science fiction, and supernatural happenings not involving God.

Submission Info: Use standard format. Prefers stories written in first person which demonstrate the good qualities and capabilities of young people. Poetry should be between 4–24 lines; stories are approximately 1,000–1,200 words long. Prefers to receive submissions in March and April.

Subscription Rates: Regular one year $3. Bonus subscription (includes C-30 YSH cassette) $5. In Canada add $4 to price.

COBBLESTONE, 20 Grove St., Peterborough, NH 03458. A monthly history magazine for young people. Monthly themes followed.

Publishes: Authentic historical and biographical fiction, adventure, retold legends, etc., relating to theme. Feature articles. Supplemental non-fiction which includes subjects directly and indirectly related to theme. Activities including crafts, recipes, woodworking projects, etc., which can be done either alone or with adult supervision. Poetry, puzzles and games. No wordfinds. Uses crosswords and other word puzzles using the vocabulary of the issue's theme. Also mazes and picture puzzles.

Submission Info: All submissions must relate to a monthly theme. Theme lists and writer's guidelines available for SASE. Refer to specific guidelines for advice on submitting a query. Pays 10–15¢ per printed word.

Editor's Remarks: "Anyone wanting to write for *Cobblestone* should first write and ask for writer's guidelines and upcoming themes."

Subscription Rates: One year: $18.95. Also available on some newsstands.

* \$ CONNECTIONS, BAT Publishing, P.O. Box 4, 245 South Brayer St., Holgate, OH 43527. Produced yearly as demand requires for writers 18 and under, and readers of any age.

Publishes: Fiction, poetry, personal experience articles from writers 18 and under. No non-fiction other than personal experience.

Submission Info: Submissions accepted *only June through December.* Fee of \$25 must accompany each submission. Writer receives one free copy. Publication comes out in spring. Acceptance acknowledged within 2 weeks with SASE. Submissions must be no more than 5 double-spaced pages, and will be edited for spelling, etc. One-time publication rights. Include name address, school, grade, etc. Individual submission fees will be waived for those submitting stories through their school's creative writing classroom group.

Editor's Remarks: "Submissions cannot be accepted without identification and submission fees. Otherwise this is a *very* open market for young writers. No photos used. This is a softcover, homemade publication that is just gaining circulation throughout American libraries and homes. We will go with the flow, producing more publications more often as demand dictates."

Subscription Rates: Available from BAT Publishing, and as a resource in public libraries. Purchase price through mail - \$5.50 (includes mailing charges).

CONTESTS & CONTACTS, P.O. Box 248, Youngtown, AZ 85363–0248. Monthly newsletter for the writer who wants to know what contests are offered, what prizes will be awarded, how to enter and win contests directed at poets and writers.

Publishes: "Poetry Pour" section has monthly contests and informative articles on the different styles of poetry. Also uses articles on how-to enter and win contests, how-to organize files and records; poetry related to the poet, contests, meeting new writers, etc.; short personal experience or news about contest winners and more.

Submission Info: Send SASE for guidelines. Sample copies \$2 plus #10 SASE.

Editor's Remarks: "We will publish free all contests directed at the poet and writer. Now the small contests that only few hear about will have a chance to ring their bells louder and give everyone a chance to enter."

Subscription Rates: One year (12 issucs) $18.

* **COUNSELOR,** Box 632, Glen Ellyn, IL 60138. Four page take-home paper for children 8 to 12 from Power/Line Papers. Christian slant.

Publishes: Greatest need is for feature length true experiences either in first or third person of youngsters who know Jesus Christ as Savior. Photo stories about activities of individual children or groups involved in interesting service projects. Our World series is short, true stories about children in other cultures who know and love Jesus Christ. Not a market for fiction, poetry, puzzles, quizzes, historical material, science and nature items, or Bible stories.

Submission Info: Feature stories should be between 900 and 1,000 words. For photo stories copy may be limited to photo captions. For our World series, stories should be between 500 and 1,000 words. Tell something about their way of life, and include graphic photos with your submission. Send SASE for detailed guidelines and free sample copies.

Editor's Remarks: "Make your short story easy to read and interesting. Without preaching, help the reader see how he may come to know Jesus Christ and/or rely on Him and His Word in everyday or unusual situations. Consider writing about adventures with pets, sports, family, friends, or school."

Subscription Rates: One year $6. Slightly higher in Canada.

* **CREATIVE KIDS MAGAZINE,** P.O. Box 6448, Mobile, AL 36660–0448. Full size magazine written expressly by gifted, creative and talented children for other children by the publishers of G/C/T, a popular magazine for parents and teachers of gifted, creative and talented children. Eight issues a year.

Publishes: Cartoons, reviews, songs, articles, puzzles, photographs, comic strips, interviews, stories, artwork, poems, activities, games, editorials, plays, computer programs, prose, etc.

Submission Info: All work must be original. Only material created by the submitter can be accepted. (This means that traced art, copied stories, and the like will not be considered.) A statement, signed and dated by the child's legal guardian or teacher attesting to the originality of each item must accompany all work. Each piece must be labeled with name, birthdate, grade, school, and home address of the child. Each child may submit as many pieces of work as desired. Illustrations, cartoons, comics, and other drawn items must be done in black ink. Only glossy finished photographs and 35mm transparencies are acceptable. Those submitting accepted material will receive a copy of the issue in which their work appears. Send for guidelines detailing specific requirements.

Editor's Remarks "We are looking for the very best material we can find by gifted, creative, and talented children to enjoy. Writers range in age from 6 to 18. Based on the pen pal page entries, the readership range is mainly 8 through 14 years old. *Creative Kids* presents a sampling of children's work that represents their ideas, questions, fears, concerns and pleasures. It does not dwell on any one aspect. The prime purpose is to encourage children to strive for a product that is good enough for publication. It requires effort, discipline, and a sense of responsibility. The reward is to know that the material has appeared in print and is shared with thousands of readers."

Subscription Rates: Available at the new reader rate of $20 per year (eight issues.)

* CREATIVE WITH WORDS, P.O. Box 223226, Carmel, CA 93922. Publishes anthologies, many of which are for or by children.

Publishes: CWW is devoted to furthering: (1) folkartistic tales and such; (2) creative writing by children (poetry, prose and language art work); (3) creative writing in special interest groups (senior citizens, handicapped, general family). Particularly interested in prose, language arts work, fillers, puzzles and poems from young people.

Submission Info: Submissions from young writers must be their own work and not edited, corrected and/or rewritten by an adult. Will work with individual young writers if editing and corrections are necessary. Do not send personal photo unless requested. Use standard format for preparing manuscripts. Poetry must be 20 lines or less. Prose should not exceed 900 words. Shorter poems and articles are always welcome. Do not send previously published material. Copyright reverts back to author after publication. No payment is made to contributors but they do receive a 20% cost reduction of publication in which their work appears. There are no copies in payment. Send SASE for return of manuscript and/or correspondence. Send SASE for current guidelines. Address submissions to: B. Geltrich.

Editor's Remarks: "CWW is an educational publication which means that it serves both the academic and non-academic communities of the world. The editors organize one annual poetry contest, offer feedback on manuscripts submitted to these contests, and publish a wide range of themes relating to human studies and the environment that influences human behaviors. CWW also critically analyzes manuscripts for minimal charge."

Subscription Rates: One year $12.

† **CROSSWINDS**, 300 East 42nd St., 6th Floor, New York, NY 10017. Publisher of books for young adults.

Publishes: Will consider young adult fiction books including mysteries and romances aimed at readers age 11–17.

Submission Info: Complete manuscripts preferred. Should be approximately 40,000 words in length. Be sure to include your name, address and phone number. Use standard format. Must be typed. Address to: Nancy Jackson. (*Author's note:* Tough market. Read what is currently being published by Crosswinds.)

† * **C.S.P. WORLD NEWS**, c/o Guy F. Claude Hamel, 1307 Bethamy Lane, Gloucester, Ontario K1J 8P3. Monthly publication with international readership.

Publishes: Particularly interested in receiving fillers, poems, and articles for various columns from young people. Open to new topics.

Submission Info: Use standard formats. Be sure to include self-addressed envelope with IRC for return postage.

Editor's Remarks: *"C.S.P. World News* has been published continually for over 25 years."

Subscription Rates: One year $18.

* DECISION, 1300 Harmon Place, Minneapolis, MN 55403. Monthly publication of the Billy Graham Evangelistic Association directed to youth and adults in every walk in life.

Publishes: Personal experience which explains how author has applied biblical principles to everyday living or crisis experience. Tell it in such a way that readers can identify and apply the same principles in similar situations in their own lives. Length: 1,800–2,000 words. Personal testimony relating author's conversion (written in first person) conveying what Christ has done in your life. Include what life was like before you became a Christian, the circumstances in which you invited Christ into your life, and what is happening at the present time. Or write another person's testimony obtained by interview or cassette tapes; also written in first person ("as told to"). Length: 1,800–2,000 words. Also uses vignettes (concise narratives relating anecdotes or incidents from life written with a spiritual application). Length: 200–1,000 words. Also poetry, free verse and occasionally rhymed poetry. Length: 4–20 lines. Payment made according to article length; poetry by word count. Send SASE for detailed guidelines for both poetry and articles. Address all material to editor: Roger C. Palms.

Editor's Remarks: "Restricted to about senior year in high school. Open to articles and poems. Material always returned. We do not have need for younger writers, either for poetry or articles. Note we are inundated with poetry."

Subscription Rates: One year $5. Send to: *Decision*, Box 779 Minneapolis, MN 55440.

* THE DETROIT FREE PRESS, Kids Book Review, 321 W. Lafayette, Detroit, MI 48231. Regional newspaper with national distribution.

Publishes: Book reviews from children, 75 word limit.

Submission Info: Include name, address, phone number, age, grade, and school. Also include the title of the book, the author, and the publisher. Pays $5 a review.

DIALOGUE, 3100 Oak Park Ave., Berwyn, IL 60402. Quarterly magazine for the visually impaired published in braille, large print, and on recorded discs playable on Talking Book machines for an audience of blind and visually impaired adults.

Publishes: Fiction and non-fiction general interest material. Photos and artwork.

Submission Info: *Dialogue* cannot consider the work of writers who are not visually impaired. Because it is a service organization, new writers are asked to include a brief statement regarding their serious visual impairment with their first submission. Freelance writer's guidelines are available in regular print, large print, braille, and on cassette. Persons wishing them on cassette should send a C-90. Sample copies are free. Be sure to request which edition you prefer. Send SASE for regular print guidelines. See guidelines for photos and artwork.

Editor's Remarks: "We write for a general interest adult audience and rarely use fiction or articles written from a juvenile point of view. A young person should study the kind of material we publish in *Dialogue* and might break into our market best with poetry or a contribution for one of our regular departments such as 'ABAPITA' or 'Vox Pop.'"

Subscription Rates: All editions—braille, large print or recorded discs for one year $30. Back copies are donated to agencies, schools, and blind individuals throughout the world."

* DOLLY MAGAZINE, 140 Joynton Avenue, Waterloo, New South Wales, Australia 2017. Entertainment, fashion, beauty magazine for girls 14–20.

Publishes: Fiction: adventure, fantasy, historical romance, humor, satire, romance, suspense with characters between the ages of 17 and

20, unmarried. Length 1,000–2,500 words. Non-fiction: Teenage interview/profile of pop stars. Length 1,000–2,500 words. Prefers teenage articles (examples include sex, drugs, diseases, decor.) Also accepts material for several departments. Pays $150 per thousand words. Accepts previously published work, computer printout submissions, though prefers letter-quality to dot-matrix. Writer's guidelines available for 23x10cm SAE plus 50¢ postage (use International Reply Coupons).

Subscription Rates: Samples available for 37x27cm SAE and $1.00 postage (use IRC). Subscription rates available, inquire with SASE.

* DRAGONFLY: EAST/WEST HAIKU QUARTERLY, Middlewood Press, P.O. Box 11236, Salt Lake City, UT 84118. Published quarterly for audience interested in haiku, Japanese literature, and nature.

Publishes: Haiku (a form of poetry) and articles about haiku.

Submission Info: Open to student submissions, and work that can be revised to meet the quality of the work we print; will often receive suggestions. Please note grade in school. Standard formats. See a current issue for more details. Sample copy is $3.50. Will also send guidelines and sample pages from past issues free for SASE if requested.

Editor's Remarks: "We publish a few students, elementary to high school grades, in every issue. Most submissions we receive from students show only a basic understanding of the form, so we strongly suggest authors read the guidelines and at least one sample copy."

Subscription Rates: In U.S. one year (four issues) $12. In Canada $14.

† EXPLORER, P.O. Box 210, Notre Dame, IN 46556. Semi-annual magazine whose subscribers and contributors come from most of the 50 states, India, Italy, Canada, the Virgin Islands and Southern Rhodesia.

Publishes: Uses all types of verse in good taste, fiction, fillers and photographs relating to travel, essays.

Submission Info: Use standard formats. Poetry: 16 lines or less. Fiction: 800 words maximum. Payment is in cash prizes from $10 to $25 based on subscriber votes. Send SASE for guidelines. Single issue copy is $3.

Subscription Info: One year (two issues) $5. Single copy $3.

† **FACES**, 20 Grove St., Peterborough, NH 03458. Monthly history magazine about people.

Publishes: Variety of feature articles and in-depth and personal accounts relating to monthly themes. Word length: 800–1,200. Also supplemental non-fiction, 200–800 words. Includes subjects directly and indirectly related to themes. Also fiction, activities, photos, poetry, puzzles and games all with a connection to theme.

Submission Info: Operates on a by-assignment basis, but welcomes ideas and suggestions in outline form. Ideas should be submitted at least 6 months prior to the publication date. Pays on individual basis. Guidelines with theme list available for SASE. Sample issue available for $3.75.

Editor's Remarks: "Writers are encouraged to study recent back issues for content and style."

Subscription Rates: Available by subscription. Write to above address.

FICTION WRITERS MONTHLY, Romantic Times Publishing Group, 163 Joralemon St., Suite 1234, Brooklyn Heights, NY 11201. How-to and industry information magazine for readers and writers of popular romance.

Publishes: Opinions and tips for and about romance writers, profiles of authors. Magazine covers paperback fiction, romance, mystery, western occult, glitz and glitter, action/adventure, science fiction, fantasy, teen fiction, etc. Occasionally covers markets for short fiction.

Submission Info: Send for a sample copy.

Subscription Rates: Six issues $30. Twelve issues $55.

* **FLIP MAGAZINE**, The Art Center, Attn: C. Fenner Williams, Editor, 265 E. Emmett St., Battle Creek, MI 49017. Published by The Art Center of Battle Creek. Aimed at young readers, writers and artists.

Publishes: Short stories, poems, essays, reviews, interviews, etc. Open to students 13 to 19. Writing on any topic is accepted for consideration. Follows special theme each issue.

Submission Info: Writers and artists should clearly identify their name, age, school and grade. Photos are not needed. Work is accepted throughout the year. Writing must be typed or clearly written, double spaced on white paper or *Flip* manuscript form which is available in the back of the magazine. Artwork should be in black and white, photos, drawings, prints are accepted. Writing may be illustrated and submitted as a package. Works are reviewed by a teen editors committee. Teens accepted for pubication receive a free copy of the magazine in which their work is published and a *Flip* T-shirt. Only work accompanied by SASE will be returned. Notification is sent to teens stating acceptance or rejection. Guidelines and upcoming themes available upon request. Sample copies available for small fee; send postcard to Art Center for rates.

Editor's Remarks: "Work most likely to be accepted is that which reflects the interests of teens."

Subscription Rates: Four issues $15. Single issues also available; send postcard for rate. Also available at subscribing libraries and schools.

† * **THE FLYING PENCIL PRESS**, P.O. Box 7667, Elgin, IL 60121. New independent publishing house dedicated to the writing and artwork of children ages 8–14.

Publishes: Compilations of children's work (fiction, non-fiction, poems, art and cartoons) in quality paperback books for the general bookstore market.

Submission Info: Prefers typewritten manuscripts but will accept handwritten material if it is clear and readable. Artwork, illustrations and cartoons should be on unlined white paper. Manuscripts must be aimed toward an upcoming theme. Material *must* be the original work of the submitting author or artist. We do not accept tracings or freehand copying of already published artwork. Writings copied from published books or magazines will not be considered. Enclose SASE if you wish material to be returned if not accepted. Be sure to keep a copy of your material in case original is lost in handling or mailing. Replies by mail in 4–6 weeks if your work is accepted. Payment may be offered. Guidelines and theme sheet available for SASE.

Editor's Remarks: "We are looking for original, honest, imaginative, bright work. Be yourself and write, draw, create from your own ideas and feelings. We hope to hear from you soon."

* FREEWAY, Box 632, Glen Ellyn, IL 60138. Publication for young Christian adults of high school or college age.

Publishes: Greatest need is for personal experience stories showing how God has worked in teens' lives. Also photos. Also accepts self-help or how-to articles with practical Christian advice on daily living, and trend articles addressing secular fads from a Christian perspective. Uses very little fiction unless it is allegory, parable, or humor.

Submission Info: Stories are best written in first person and "as told to" author. Use standard format. Computer printouts okay. Incorporate specific details, anecdotes and dialogue. Limit manuscripts to 1,000 words or less. Prefers black and white photos, but will consider clearly defined color prints if the colors are bluish rather than reddish. Photos should be at least 5 x 7″ but will accept snapshots or Polaroids if they are sharp and clear. Payments vary: all rights bring 6–10¢ per word (but will forward total reprint fees to author if material is reprinted by another publisher); first rights bring 4–7¢ per word; second rights 3–5¢. Black and white photos $5 to $20; color transparencies and prints bring $5–$35. Send SASE for a special "Tips to Writers" pamphlet and free sample copy.

Editor's Remarks: "Photographs are an important and often essential part of our true stories. When submitting please indicate the subject's current address, at least two references (his pastor could be one), a note signed by the subject stating that he has reviewed your story and is willing to have it published (or a similar note from parents of a child under 18.) Study our samples carefully, then query or submit complete manuscript."

Subscription Rates: One year $6.25. Slightly higher in Canada.

* FUTURIFIC MAGAZINE, 280 Madison Avenue, New York, NY

10016. Published 12 times a year by Futurific, Inc., a not-for-profit educational organization dedicated to finding a better understanding of the future. Not related to any other organization, corporate, governmental, religious or otherwise.

Publishes: Material that is an analysis of any issue in current events. All material must show what *improvements* are coming in the near future. No gloom and doom stories, and do not try to tell readers how they should live their lives. Wants material which tells what *will* happen.

Submission Info: Buys one-time rights. Payment is negotiated. Material will only be returned with SASE. Presently only black and white photos and artwork are used. Sample copies available for $5, which includes processing, postage and handling.

Editor's Remarks: "Readership consists of anyone interested in the future and who is uncomfortable at the lack of research dealing with it and the lack of accurate foresight available. We are only interested in how correct you are in reporting on the future. Fantasy must be wed to reality. Remember, we are not as interested in your age as your correct view of where the world is heading."

Subscription Rates: One year for individuals $30; institutions $60.

* GRIT, 208 West Third St., Williamsport, PA 17701. Tabloid-size national weekly newspaper for all ages. General readership in small-town rural America.

Publishes: Well-written articles about individuals and groups who are making an important contribution to their neighbors, community, and/or the American way of life. Also interested in patriotic articles having an immediate tie-in with a date. Articles can be about men and women of all ages, teenagers and children. Also uses articles about religion, such as how churches raise money or develop successful programs that are unusual and set them apart from other congregations, and about the spirit of a community. In addition, "Family of the Week" features a focus on families who have shared an exciting adventure, overcome adversity or shown unusual creativity.

Submission Info: Handwritten copy is not acceptable. Manuscripts must be typed. Send statement verifying that manuscript is original work of writer. Limit articles to between 300–500 words. With few exceptions, articles should be accompanied by good-quality black and white photos or color transparencies with captions identifying people, objects, and telling accurately what is happening. Always include SASE when submitting any manuscripts, photos, or other material requiring a reply. Pays on acceptance. Writer's guidelines are free. Sample copies will be sent for $1 to cover postage and handling.

Editor's Remarks: "Stories should be about specific individuals doing admirable things successfully. They should show the value of honesty, thrift, hard work, generosity and other positive attributes as keys to better living. Find a theme, whatever the subject, so that you will have a story to submit. Write of someone's unusual contribution to family, community, school, church, etc. as concisely and interestingly as you can; don't send us a biographical profile or a dull compilation of information."

Subscription Rates: Write to above address. Also available on many newsstands nationwide.

* HIGHLIGHTS FOR CHILDREN, 803 Church St., Honesdale, PA 18431. Published monthly for youngsters ages 2 to 12.

Publishes: Accepts poems, drawings, and stories from readers. Also runs four unfinished stories a year to which readers submit their creative endings. For writers 16 or older; also reviews submissions of short stories, factual features, party plans, crafts, finger plays, and action plays. Seldom buys verse.

Submission Info: For writers up to age 15, make drawings in black and white. For a special feature, "Creatures Nobody Has Ever Seen," drawings are sent in color. Prose usually run no more than 250 words. Acknowledges all material submitted. However, material is not returned, so *do not enclose SASE*. No payment is made for contributions from writers 15 or under. For writers over 16, consult regular freelance guidelines available free. Fiction should not be more than 900 words; pays 8¢ and up per word. Science and factual articles within 900 words bring $75 and up. Other material brings $25 and up. Those 16 and over should send complete manuscript with SASE for its possible return. All submissions need to include name, age, and complete home address. Personal photo is unnecessary.

Subscription Rates: One year $19.95. Three years $49.95. Write: *Highlights for Children*, 2300 West Fifth Avenue, P.O. Box 269, Columbus, OH 43216.

HONOLULU THEATRE FOR YOUTH, Box 3257, Honolulu, HI 96801. HTY is a professional non-profit regional theatre company.

Publishes: Accepts stories for production and pays royalty for scripts that are accepted.

Submission Info: Scripts may be submitted anytime; reading and reply period is 6 to 9 months. Scripts should be suitable for production by adults on themes of interest to young people. Small casts, simple technical requirements are important considerations in choosing a script for production.

Editor's Remarks: "Honolulu Theatre for Youth is a leading American theatre for young audiences. It plays to 145,000 people annually— state-wide in Hawaii—and also tours in the Pacific Basin and occasionally to the Mainland U.S. Plays produced by HTY receive wide national recognition in theatre publications."

* HUMPTY DUMPTY'S MAGAZINE, 1100 Waterway Blvd., P.O. Box 567, Indianapolis, IN 46206. Monthly publication for children ages 4 to 6 from the Children's Better Health Institute. Stresses health-related themes or ideas including nutrition, safety, exercise, or proper health habits.

Publishes: From readers: artwork or pictures drawn or colored by the readers themselves.

Submission Info: Send drawn or colored pictures or other artwork. Include SASE if you wish material not accepted to be returned. No payment is made for published reader material. All contributors may purchase copies in which their work appears at a reduced rate. Sample copies available for 75¢. Submissions should be limited to children ages 4–6.

Editor's Remarks: "Unfortunately, because of the many thousands of contributions we receive, we are not able to publish everything sent in to us. We do hope that parents and teachers explain to the children that failure to get their pictures published does not mean that the artwork wasn't well done. It simply means that we didn't have room."

Subscription Rates: One year $11.95. Special rate of $9.97 is usually offered in every issue.

* IN TOUCH, Box 50434, Indianapolis, IN 46250. Weekly magazine published in conjunction with the Aldersgate Graded Curriculum to reinforce each week's session.

Publishes: Non-fiction including Christian testimonies, observations on contemporary issues, how-to articles, humor, interviews with famous or newsworthy Christians. Fiction needs include a true experience told in fiction style, humorous fiction, or a C.S. Lewis-type allegory. Does not use poetry, cartoons or puzzles.

Submission Info: Length for both fiction and non-fiction is 500–1,500 words. Send seasonal material at least nine months in advance. Manuscripts need to be typed. Be sure to include word count. Indicate what rights are being offered: one-time, simultaneous, or reprint. Usually buys one-time rights. Pays 2–3¢ a word for first rights; 2¢ a word for reprints. Photos are purchased separately from $15–$25. Sample copy and guidelines available for SASE.

Editor's Remarks: "Include photos if available. We need *Seventeen* and *Campus Life* type cover shots and close-ups of faces. We do not need teens sitting in meadows reading Bibles in soft focus. Understand the official *In Touch* password: 'Wesleyan-Arminian-evangelical-holiness manuscript.' Roughly translated that means articles should reflect a joy and excitement in a personal relationship with God . . . We attempt to encourage a biblical lifestyle, witnessing, sexual purity, and abstinence from all things harmful to the body and soul, without being 'preachy.'"

* JACK AND JILL, 1100 Waterway Blvd., P.O. Box 567, Indianapolis, IN 46206. Monthly publication for children ages 6 to 8 from the Children's Better Health Institute. Stresses health-related themes or ideas including nutrition, safety, exercise, or proper health habits.

Publishes: From readers: interesting letters, jokes and riddles, original stories and articles, original poetry, book reviews and artwork.

Submission Info: Prefers stories and poems that are typed with double-spacing but will also accept contributions that are written legibly in ink. Put your name, age, school and complete address on each page of your work. Stories and articles may be up to 500 words. Include SASE if you wish material to be returned if not accepted. No payment is made for published reader material. All contributors may purchase copies in which their work appears at a reduced rate. Send SASE for guidelines. Sample copies available for 75¢. Submissions should be limited to young people ages 6–8.

Editor's Remarks: "Unfortunately, because of the many thousands of contributions we receive, we are not able to publish everything sent in to us."

Subscription Rates: One year $11.95. Special rate of $9.97 is usually offered in every issue.

† * **JUNIOR EDITOR,** 709 S.E. 52nd Avenue, Ocala, FL 32671. Magazine featuring material written by all ages of students except those in college. Published monthly.

Publishes: Variety of material including poems, short stories, non-fiction, fillers, essays, etc. Also accepts black and white ink drawings.

Submission Info: Perfers manuscripts that are no longer than 1½ single-spaced typed pages. (Note: That is approximately 3 pages double-spaced.) Will also consider manuscripts that are neatly handwritten. Drawings may be up to 8″ x 10″ in size. Include name, age, address, school, grade and teacher's name with submission. Do not send photos. Tries to respond within 2–3 weeks. Retains all rights. Does not return submissions. Magazine is copyrighted. Students whose work is accepted receive a tearsheet of their published material. Sample copies available for $1 to cover postage. Guidelines included in each issue. One free copy available to any interested teacher or librarian. Address submissions to Susie Pettrey, Editor or Florence F. Bradley, Editor.

Editor's Remarks: "We like 3–4 poems to choose from. We try to publish at least one piece from each contributor. We are especially looking for work from students in grades 5 through high school. Submissions from an entire class are encouraged."

Subscription Rates: One year for teachers $10. One year for others $20.

* **KOALA CLUB NEWS**, Zoological Society of San Diego, Inc., P.O. Box 551, San Diego, CA 92112. Quarterly publication for children age 15 and under.

Publishes: Accepts original drawings, black and white photos, poems, riddles and stories for "Porky Pine's Pen Pals" section. The material must be about animals.

Submission Info: Use standard format. No submissions returned. No payment is made for accepted submissions, but will send a free *Zoo Babies* book to young writers whose submissions are published. Include name, age and address with each submission. Write with SASE for information about obtaining a sample copy.

Subscription Rates: *Koala Club News* is available to members of the Society's Koala Club. Membership dues of $9 per year include unlimited entrance to the San Diego Zoo, the San Diego Wild Animal Park, and the quarterly publication.

† * **LIFEPRINTS**, P.O. Box 5181, Salem, OR 97304. (503) 581–4224. Published five times annually by Blindskills, Inc., a non-profit organization for visually-impaired adults and youth. Available in large print, braille and cassette. Has international readership.

Publishes: Career, sports, and leisure articles, topics of interest to students—fashion, study skills, social skills, book reviews—and notices about technology and other aids available to visually-impaired persons, and personal experience pieces by visually-impaired adults and youth.

Submission Info: *All* submissions must written by visually-impaired individuals. Interested young people are urged to study a sample copy in either large print, braille or cassette. Visually-impaired adults write on a volunteer basis. Visually-impaired students who submit articles which are published receive a small honorarium from monies donated for that purpose. Sample copy available for $3; specify format desired.

Brochure available for SASE to all persons interested in learning more about *Lifeprints*.

Editor's Remarks: "Our emphasis is on experiential articles and methods used by successful visually-impaired students and adults. We welcome submissions from middle and high school, as well as college youth. *Lifeprints* is a role model publication which, by example, inspires its readers to realize their vocational and selected lifestyle potential. We don't have printed guidelines. It's best to study a sample issue."

Subscription Rates: Subscription/donation of $15 is suggested annually.

* LISTEN, JOURNAL OF BETTER LIVING, 6830 Laurel Street NW, Washington, D.C. 20012. A monthly publication for teens and young adults encouraging the development of good habits and high ideals of physical and mental health.

Publishes: Special column for teens called "Graffiti" which uses short, well-written, thought-provoking poems, stories, and essays from teen writers. Also uses factual features or opinion essays with or without accompanying quality photos; narratives based on true-life incidents, poetry, puzzles, and cartoons.

Submission Info: Submissions for "Graffiti" should include age, grade, school, etc; no photos. Poetry should not be longer than 20 lines; stories and essays 300–500 words. Address to "Graffiti" in care of *Listen* magazine. Include SASE. Send for free writer's guidelines and tip sheet. Samples available for $1 and large manila envelope with SASE. Pays $10 for poems; $15–$20 for stories and essays. Varying rates for other material.

Editor's Remarks: "*Listen* is circulated in public high schools and junior high schools, so religious material is not suitable."

Subscription Rates: One year (12 monthly issues) $11.95. Higher outside U.S. Send check of money order to *Listen*, P.O. Box 7000, Boise, ID 83707. Also available in many school libraries.

* THE MCGUFFEY WRITER, 400A McGuffey Hall, Miami University, Oxford, OH 45056. Magazine of children's own writing published three times a year for a nationwide audience.

Publishes: Short stories, essays, poems and songs. Also cartoons and illustrations done in black and white. Each issue follows a predetermined theme. Open to students K–12.

Submission Info: Manuscripts submitted will be acknowledged but are not returned. (You do not need to enclose SASE.) Students must list name, grade level, school, and address on every submitted page. Do not include photo. A teacher, supervisor or responsible adult must sign the initial page for verification. Typed or handwritten submissions are equally welcome as long as they are readable; however, the child's original copy is preferable. Due to limited space, excerpts may be taken from work that is longer than two double-spaced typewritten pages. Guidelines available at the above address. Sample copies are $2 each. Guidelines, helpful hints, and deadlines are given in each issue.

Editor's Remarks: "Items are accepted on the basis of merit, originality and appropriateness to the overall balance and theme of the issue."

Subscription Rates: One year single subscription (3 issues: Fall, Winter, Spring) $5. Institutional rates (for three complete yearly subscriptions sent to a single address) $10. For one year patron subscription (helps to defray costs) send $15. Patrons are listed on the inside of the spring issue.

* MERLYN'S PEN, The National Magazine of Student Writing. P.O. Box 1058, East Greenwich, RI 02818. Toll free: (800) 247-2027, in RI (401) 885-5175. Magazine written entirely by students in grades 7–10. Four issues published during school year.

Publishes: Stories, plays, poems, reviews, letters, word games, reviews, opinions, essays on important issues (take a stand!), critiques of writing in magazine, and art by students in grades 7–10. Also considers word games and puzzles. Letters to the editor are welcome.

Submission Info: A statement of originality must be signed for each accepted piece. Published authors and artists receive 3 complimentary issues which contain their work and a small gift. Guidelines for submitting literature and art must be followed exactly. Each submission receives a response within 12 weeks. All submissions (art and literature) *must** include a large, self-addressed stamped envelope; a cover sheet with author's name, grade, age, home address, home phone number, school name, school address, school phone, and supervising teacher's name. Manuscripts must be typed, double-spaced, with extra-wide margins. Manuscripts should be stapled and the author's name should be on every page. Artwork should be in black ink or charcoal on white paper (no lead pencil or blue ink). Color work (oils, pastels, watercolor, etc.) can only be considered for the cover. Photographs should be shot with a 35mm camera; 8″ x 10″ glossy prints are preferred. Art work should not be folded or matted, but cardboard backing in envelope should be used. Include all necessary information (see * above) and SASE with adequate postage. No personal photos necessary.

Editor's Remarks: *"Merlyn's Pen* considers all kinds of literature written by students in grades 7–10. The magazine seeks manuscripts that grip the readers' interest and stir the heart and mind. The best advice we can offer is: Write what *you* know and revise, revise, revise! Make every word count!"

Subscription Rates: 1987–88 rates for one year (four issues during school year) $9.95 each for 1–4 subscriptions; $7.95 each (5–10 subscriptions); $5.85 each (11–20 subs); $4.95 each (21 or more subs).

† **MICHIGAN NATURAL RESOURCES MAGAZINE,** Box 30034, Lansing, MI 48909. Bi-monthly publication which highlights Michigan's many natural resources and promotes reader appreciation and respect of same.

Publishes: Queries or completed manuscripts on Michigan subjects of conservation and environmental protection, how-to articles about the outdoors, and topics that will interest our statewide readership. Does not publish cartoons, puzzles or fillers. Only uses poems on rare occasions and are primarily oriented to outdoor articles with a strong Michigan flavor.

Submission Info: Use standard format. Include social security number on all queries and manuscripts. Manuscripts should be from 1,500 to 3,000 words. Include a biographical sketch with cover letter. When possible, also attach a bibliography of the subject on which you are writing. Prefers 35mm slides for photos. Must be in razor sharp focus and not be duplicates. Send SASE with all submissions. Address all submissions to: Mr. Norris R. McDowell at above address. Send SASE for detailed guidelines. Sample issues available for $3 (or check your local library).

Editor's Remarks: "Though *not* a youth-oriented magazine, we would be delighted to take a look at a young person's submission."

Subscription Rates: Available at most Michigan libraries. Write to above address for subscription information.

* NATIONAL GEOGRAPHIC WORLD, National Geographic Society, 1145 17th NW, Washington, DC 20036. A monthly picture magazine for readers age 8 and older.

Publishes: Children's art, photographs, or games.

Subscription Info: *World* is a highly specialized market for regular photos and text. Read several back issues. Send SASE for specific guidelines before submitting any material. Pays $10 for children's contributions of art, photographs, or games published. All contributors receive 3 complimentary copies of the issue in which their work appears. Additional copies may be purchased at a reduced rate.

Editor's Remarks: "*World* editors will *not* review poetry, fiction, manuscripts, or story proposals unaccompanied by acceptable pictures."

Subscription Rates: Available through National Geographic Society.

* OUR FAMILY, Box 249, Battleford, Saskatchewan, Canada S0M 0E0. Monthly magazine published for a national readership of Catholic families, most of whom have children in grade school, high school or college.

Publishes: Non-fiction relating to the following areas: people at home; people in relation to God; people at recreation; people at work; people in the world; biography (profiles about Christians whose living of

Christian values has had a positive effect on their contemporaries); and inspirational articles. Also spiritual reflection; humorous anecdotes; poetry on human/spiritual themes; cartoons (family-type); photos. Also fiction aimed primarily at the 18–40 age bracket.

Subscription Info: Send for detailed guidelines for non-fiction, fiction, and photos by enclosing SAE and 42¢ Canadian postage or IRC. Sample copy is $1.50.

Editor's Remarks: "The majority of our readers are adults. If young people write for us, they must understand that they are writing and competing in an adult market. Since our publication stresses the personal experience approach, young people could find a slot in our publication by writing as teenagers focusing on teenage concerns. We make no distinction of age. If a particular article/poem/filler effectively reaches a certain segment of the family, we are pleased to purchase it for publication on our magazine."

* OWLFLIGHT, Unique Graphics, 1025 55th St., Oakland, CA 94608. Publishes science fiction and fantasy for a multi-generational group of people.

Publishes: Short stories 3,000 to 8,000 words and poems 8 to 100 lines.

Subscription Info: Send #10 SAE with 39¢ postage for detailed guidelines which will include information on what *Owlflight*'s current writing and art needs are, as well as current subscription rates. For sample copy, enclose $2.50 instead of SASE with your guideline request.

Editor's Remarks: "If unfamiliar with our publication do not submit anything until you have seen the guidelines. We are not looking for writing or art from a particular age group, but for work that can be judged on its own merit. Most of our contributors range from high school age through senior citizens, but the youngest was ten when she wrote a story published in *Owlflight*. I try to be gentle and constructive when I must reject something, so please *do not* tell me your age when submitting anything. I will not buy something because it was good for someone that age to have written, if it wouldn't have been good enough if written by an adult. (One of the best stories in a recent professional anthology, *Sword & Sorceress II*, edited by Marion Zimmer Bradley, was by a 17 year old; Jane Gaskell and Samuel R. Delaney are among many writers in fantasy or science fiction who published novels while in their teens. Other first novelists have been over fifty.")

Subscription Rates: Send SASE for current subscription rates.

PEOPLE IN ACTION, 1720 Washington Blvd., P.O. Box 10010, Ogden, UT 84409.

Publishes: Feature stories on people around the country, in various careers and lifestyles who are doing interesting and unusual things; winning, overcoming, helping others and enjoying life. Cover stories feature celebrities in all fields: art, entertainment, communications, business, science and technology. A regular feature is the celebrity chef column which includes a profile on and recipe of an interesting person who is also a gourmet cook.

Subscription Info: Articles should run about 1,200 words and be accompanied by color transparencies to illustrate the piece. Celebrity chef column should be between 500–700 words, with accompanying color transparencies. (Does not use recipes containing alcoholic spirits.) Query first with SASE to Fern Porras. Send SASE for writer's and photographer's guidelines.

Editor's Remarks: "We are not a subscription or newsstand magazine. Our magazines are purchased by businesses, physicians, banks, realtors, etc. as advertising vehicles for them to send to their customers and clients."

THE POETRY REVIEW, Poetry Society of America, 15 Gramercy Park South, New York, NY 10003. A semi-annual literary magazine open to both members and non-members.

Publishes: Poetry, essays, and translations by PSA members and non-members. Unsolicited manuscripts welcome.

Subscription Info: Address manuscripts to the Editor, *The Poetry Review*, in care of the PSA offices. For detailed information regarding all PSA activities, send SASE to the above address.

Subscription Rates: Single issue $3; annual subscription $5.

* PRISM, 1040 Bayview Drive Suite 210, Ft. Lauderdale, FL 33304. Publishes six issues September through May for gifted and talented young people ages 10 to 18.

Publishes: Poetry, short stories, plays, etc. Also artwork and photos.

Subscription Info: Double space submissions. Encourages photos and artwork sent to accompany submission, sometimes incorporated into story. Note age and school attended along with your telephone number. Print name and address. Payment is in copies. No acknowledgment of submission is made. However, all original artwork is returned. Sample copy is $4.

Editor's Remarks: "Students should request a sample copy of *Prism* to get a feel for our publication, but it is not required to submit works. Please note age and school attended along with a phone number with submission. Our Editor likes to chat. We especially need artwork from young people."

Subscription Rates: One year (six issues published September to May) $19.95. Also available through magazine agencies. For subscription write: *Prism Magazine*, P.O. Box 030464, Ft. Lauderdale, FL 33303-0464.

* PURPLE COW, Signa Publications, 3423 Piedmont Rd. N.E., Ivy Place Suite 320, Atlanta, GA 30305. Monthly tabloid (10 issues) covering any subject of interest to 13 to 18 year olds.

Publishes: General articles of interest to teens; book, movie and record reviews; humor; interview/profile; sports (general and anecdotal— no "How to Play Soccer"); personal experience; coping with problems (drugs, sex, etc.); and seasonal interest material. Also needs filler material.

Subscription Info: All manuscripts must be typed and accompanied by SASE. Articles should be between 500–3,000 words. Pays $5–$40. Maximum length for fillers is 150 words. Pays $5–$10 for fillers and photos. Send complete manuscript or query with published clips of published work. Buys one-time rights. Submit seasonal and holiday material 3 months in advance. Simultaneous, photocopied, and previously published submissions are okay. Sample copy sent for $1. Pays on acceptance. Address to: Margaret Anthony, Editor.

Editor's Remarks: "We are written about 80% by high school students. Know what you're talking about. Don't talk down. Have something new to say."

Subscription Rates: Distributed free to middle and high school students in metro Atlanta area.

†* **REFLECTIONS,** Dean Harper, Editor, P.O. Box 368, Duncan Falls, OH 43734. National poetry magazine published by 7th and 8th graders for students of all ages. Published in May and January of each year.

Publishes: Poetry, short stories, essays, plays, teaching ideas, humorous articles, and interviews. Also uses 8″ x 10″ color glossy photos for cover photos.

Subscription Info: Manuscripts may be hand-written if they are legible, typed or computer printed. Include your name, age, school, address, and your teacher's name. Be sure to include SASE with manuscript. Make the statement that this is your own original work, then date it and sign your name. Your teacher or parent should also sign statement. Acceptance is normally made within ten days. Send SASE for more information. Sample copies for $2. Payment is contributor's copy.

Editor's Remarks: "Including your age is helpful. Sending a personal photo is okay. Each issue contains approximately 50 poems, at least one short story, and an interview with a poet or a featured writing program."

Subscription Rates: One year (two issues) $5. One issue $3. Back issues $2.

* **RHYME TIME POETRY NEWSLETTER**, P.O. Box 1870, Hayden, ID 83835. Bimonthly poetry publication.

Publishes: Short seasonal poetry, preferably rhymed. Also poetry that does not relate to the seasons. Some free verse. Does not use haiku, avant-garde or shaped poems. Small drawings in India ink are used.

Subscription Info: Type carefully; avoid colored paper and hard-to-read type. Skip exclamation marks!! Poems must not be longer than 16 lines. Reports in one month; one time rights used. Payment is copies. Always enclose SASE. Sample copy and guidelines free with SASE and two first class stamps.

Editor's Remarks: "Be sure your rhyme and meter are consistent. Count on your fingers if necessary. Writing poetry is like being pregnant—you have to plan nine months in advance. Don't send us poems for the current season. Do not include extraneous material—we don't care about the poet's age or education. Just send your best work, with a SASE."

Subscription Rates: One year $7.50.

* SCHOLASTIC SCOPE, Student Writing, 730 Broadway, New York, NY 10003.

Publishes: Poems, stories, plays, and mini-mysteries from readers for its Student Writing pages.

Subscription Info: Please type or print your contribution, and sign a statement saying: "This is my original work; it is not a copy of someones else's work. I understand that if it is published in *Scholastic Scope*, it becomes the property of Scholastic, Inc." Have your teacher or parents sign it, too. Due to the overwhelming number of student contributions, manuscripts are no longer acknowledged by mail. If your contribution is selected for publication, you will be notified. Manuscript will be returned only if SASE is enclosed. Address manuscript to Student Writing, *Scholastic Scope.*

Editor's Remarks: "Please note that stories and plays of under ten pages have a better chance of being published in *Scope* than longer ones."

* SEVENTEEN, 850 Third Avenue, New York, NY 10022. Monthly magazine for teens.

Publishes: Articles for "Your Words" are usually personal experience. Your piece may deal with a hobby, travel adventure, sports feature, school-related subject—any topic you think will interest readers of

Seventeen. "Your Opinion" articles express a view on a timely, debatable topic. The writer takes a stand and develops an argument. Your best writing will reflect personal experience. The "You Said It" department is a potpourri of poems, hobby ideas, practical tips, book reviews, humorous observations and comments, or news about a local happening.

Subscription Info: Manuscripts should be typed using standard format. Enclose SASE. For "Your Words" articles it is best to check with the editor to be sure a similar article to the one you have planned hasn't been done recently. Word limit is 2,000. Payment for "Your Opinion" articles is $100. Short poems are preferred but will consider poems up to 40 lines in length. Do not submit more than 5 poems at one time. All material must be original. Send SASE for complete guidelines for teen writers.

Editor's Remarks: "*Seventeen* welcomes original contributions by young writers. Writers for Teen Features should be no older than twenty-one."

Subscription Rates: Available on newsstands and by subscription.

† * **SHOE TREE: The Literary Magazine by and for Young Writers**, The National Association for Young Writers, P.O. Box 452, Belvidere, NJ 07823. * Published three times a year. Featuring writings and art by children ages 6 to 14.

Publishes: Stories, poems, narrative essays, book reviews, and artwork by children.

Subscription Info: You must be between ages 6 and 14 to submit material. No restrictions on length of manuscripts. Longer stories will appear in installments if necessary. Paintings and drawings are accepted in any color or size. Children interested in illustrating poems and stories should send samples of their work. Those interested in writing book reviews should first send a query letter to Editor Sheila Cowing. Send SASE for guidelines. Work to be returned must also be accompanied by SASE. Reporting time: 8–10 weeks. Payment made in copies. Sample copies available for $5.00.

Editor's Remarks: "We encourage children to draw on their own experiences when writing stories, but also occasionally welcome well-written fantasy pieces. Humorous stories and poems are also a favorite. *Editor's Note:* Send all submissions to: *Shoe Tree*'s editorial office at 215 Valle del Sol, Santa Fe, NM 87501.

Subscription Rates: Available to public and school libraries through most major subscription services. Individual subscriptions are available directly from the publisher. One year $15. Two years $28. Three years $42.

$ SHORT STORY REVIEW, Trouvere Company, Rt. 2 Box 290, Eclectic, AL 36024. Features the short story form. Published 3 times a year.

Publishes: Short stories, 500–3,000 words, any subject, by subscribers only. Also uses articles by subscribers and *non-subscribers* about short stories or related to short stories. Maximum length 1,000 words.

Subscription Info: Send SASE for specific guidelines. Uses original manuscript to photocopy story. *Single space* leaving a one-inch margin on all sides. Use small type (15 or 12 pitch) unless you only have large. If you *do not* want your address to appear, leave it off the manuscript.

Editor's Remarks: "This publication is for subscribers only because its purpose is to learn about short story writing. Therefore short stories are only accepted by active members. Each issue will contain short stories and articles about short story writing. One of the main concepts of this working paper is to help in the improvement of writing better short stories. Along with the helpful articles will be a questionnaire on each individual article and short story. Answered honestly and constructively we will compile the information to give an overall look at each piece. This is a working paper. Each subscriber will be qualified to have *at least* two short stories printed per year."

Subscription Rates: Membership subscription $12 per year (3 issues: March, July, November.) Sample copy or extra copies $3.

* SPINOFF, Gifted Children Monthly, P.O. Box 115, Sewell, NJ 08080. Special multi-page insert in publication for gifted and talented children ages 4 to 14.

Publishes: A wide variety of material including original puzzles, tricks, mazes, challenges, stories, poems, essays, and word games. Also uses photos and artwork.

Subscription Info: Most submissions should be for one of the regular departments. Special guidelines for young writers arc in each issue. Sample for 9 x 12″ SASE. Manuscripts are not returned except for artwork and photos, which require SASE. Contributors receive $1–$3 or quality prizes for each item used unless otherwise noted.

Editor's Remarks: "Be sure your submission is directed toward a particular department. Study a few issues."

Subscription Rates: One year $24. Write GCM, P.O.Box 7200, Bergenfield, NJ 07621.

SPORTS PARADE, 1720 Washington Blvd., P.O. Box 10010, Ogden, UT 84409.

Publishes: Covers the entire spectrum, from the National Football League to horseshoes with emphasis 2 to 1 in favor of spectator sports over participation. Uses personality profiles on current stars and yesterday's heroes who are still living; sports humor; and the unusual.

Subscription Info: Articles should run about 1,200 or 1,500 words and should be accompanied by color transparencies to illustrate the piece. Query with SASE associate editor, Brent Israelson, first before submitting manuscript. Send SASE for article and photo guidelines.

Editor's Remarks: "We are not a subscriber or newsstand magazine. Our magazines are purchased by businesses, physicians, banks, realtors, etc. as advertising vehicles for them to send to their customers and clients."

* STICKERS & STUFF, Ira Friedman, Inc., 10 Columbus Circle, Suite 1300, New York, NY 10019. Published quarterly for kids between the ages of 6–14. Formerly *Stickers!* magazine.

Publishes: Short articles about the following sticker-related areas: the companies that make products, kids who collect them, related activities. "Stickerama" is a regular short new section. Every issue includes games, activities and contests. Has special "Junior Editor" column that asks for reader submissions on any topic.

Subscription Info: Writers (young and old) must query the editor, Bob Woods, first at the above address explaining the type of article you would like to submit. Replies within 4 weeks. All submissions must be typed, double-spaced. Include SASE with queries. Writer's guidelines and sample copy are available on request. Buys First North American rights.

Editor's Remarks: "*Stickers & Stuff* is a children's magazine, but we have always written on a rather adult level. That is, we do not talk down to our readers. We realize the wide range of reading abilities of children this age (6–14) but we try to make the material challenging, entertaining and educational. We don't mind sending readers to the dictionary or to a parent for help in getting through an issue. At the same time, there is plenty in each issue to keep the youngest reader thrilled."

Subscription Rates: Available nationally on newsstands, in toy stories (Toys R Us,) book stores (Waldenbooks,) gift and stationery stores, supermarkets, etc. Also available by subscription: $10 per year. Sent to: *Stickers & Stuff*, P.O. Box 166, Dept. 27, Mt. Morris, IL 61054.

* STONE SOUP, The Magazine by Children, The Children's Art Foundation, Box 83, Santa Cruz, CA 95063. A magazine written entirely by children and published five times a year (Sept., Nov., Jan., March, May.)

Publishes: Stories, poems, book reviews, and art by children up to age 13.

Subscription Info: All work must be accompanied by SASE. Reporting time is 8 weeks. Payment made in copies and discounts. Guidelines are available upon request.

Editor's Remarks: "Children interested in reviewing books should write Gerry Mandel for more information. Let her know the kind of book you like to read. Children interested in illustrating should send two samples of their artwork. We prefer stories to poems, and we especially like stories for which children draw their inspiration from real life.

We do not like formula writing of any kind (e.g., haunted house stories, take-offs on movies or TV, rhyming poems, haiku, cinquain, etc.)."

Subscription Rates: One year $19. Two years $33. Three years $45.

* STRAIGHT, 8121 Hamilton Avenue, Cincinnati, OH 45231. Published quarterly for Christian teens, ages 13–19. Distributed through churches, youth organizations and private subscriptions.

Publishes: Poetry, stories, and articles from teens. Material must be religious/inspirational in nature and appeal to other teens. Art and photos accepted occasionally.

Subscription Info: Submit manuscript on speculation, enclose SASE, birthdate (day and year), and Social Security number. Reports in 4–6 weeks. Buys first and one-time rights; pays 2¢ per word. Samples automatically sent to contributors. Guidelines and sample issues available for SASE. Artwork must be black pen on white paper only, no pencil, marker or crayon. Black and white 8″ x 10″ glossies preferred. Photos bring $15–$25 for first use, and $10–$15 for re-use. Rates for teen submissions vary.

Editor's Remarks: "Before you submit, please get to know us. Most teen work that I reject does not fit our editorial slant (religious/inspirational). A look at our guidelines or a sample copy will help teen writers in deciding what to submit. Also, I'd like to encourage teens to write about things they know, but not necessarily 'common' or general topics. We see scores of poems about rainbows and loneliness and friends, but hardly any about 'How I feel about working at McDonalds, 'What happened when I tried something new . . . ,' or 'Why I believe in . . . .' Also a tacked-on moral does not make a religious story. Make your *characters* Christian, and the religious slant will take care of itself."

* SUNSHINE MAGAZINE, P.O. Box 40, Sunshine Park, Litchfield, IL 62056. Published by Henrichs Publications, Inc. Targeted to the whole family. Special features for and by young people.

Publishes: Inspirational fiction and essays. Also some poems. Uses two or three short items by young writers in each issue. One page in each issue is devoted to pen pals for young people.

Subscription Info: Submit all material to the editor. A photo is not necessary, but please tell us your age. There is no payment for short items by young people, but authors receive complimentary copies. Always send SASE with submission. Reports in 2 months. Payment varies for other submissions. Pays on acceptance.

Editor's Remarks: "We're always eager to hear from young writers with short poems and articles under 150 words. Our guidelines give more specifics, but a sample copy would best give young writers an idea of what we are looking for."

Subscription Rates: One year $9. Two years $17. Three years $25. Quantity rates available.

* TEEN POWER, Box 632, Glen Ellyn, IL 60138. Eight-page weekly magazine for junior high Christain teens.

Publishes: How-to (issues of Christian maturity); personal experience stories showing how God has worked in teens' lives; interviews and profiles of Christian personalities; inspirational pieces for young teens. Does not accept reviews or non-Christian oriented material. Accepts photos with true story manuscripts only. Fiction must have teen Christian slant.

Subscription Info: Stories are best written from first person and "as told to" author. Submit typed manuscripts, double-spaced, include name, address, Social Security number and approximate word count. Computer printouts okay. Try to incorporate specific details, anecdotes and dialogue. Limit manuscripts to 1,000 words; shorter pieces preferred. Send black and white photos or clearly defined color prints. Payments vary: All rights bring 6–10¢ a word (but will forward total reprint fees to author if material is reprinted by another publisher); first rights bring 4–7¢; second rights bring 3–5¢ a word. Buys photos for between $5–$35 depending on quality and type. Send SASE for a special "Tips to Writers' pamphlet and free sample copy.

Editor's Remarks: "Model your true story after the examples in a sample copy. Use first person 'I', focus around one central idea or incident."

Subscription Rates: One year $6.25. Slightly higher in Canada.

* TEENAGE, *Teenage Magazine,* 217 Jackson St., Box 948, Lowell, MA 01853. A national news and entertainment magazine written for ages 14 to 19. Articles address teenagers in a mature way and contain material relevant to young people concerned with today's issues and trends.

Publishes: Features on serious, service-oriented topics as they relate to teenagers on a national level, interviews with famous people including movie and TV stars, musicians and sports figures. Profiles of teenagers who are exceptionally unique, talented or resourceful. Material for columns: Mind and Body, College, Careers, Money, and Wheels. Uses original short stories. Accepts essays and opinions for "Frontline" column by students 21 or younger. Also uses some filler material. Does *not* accept any poetry or juvenile romances.

Subscription Info: Features should be between 1,500 and 2,000 words; profiles between 400 and 1,500 words. Payment is arranged on individual basis, but can range from $100 to $1,000 upon publication. Address submissions to Attn: Feature Editor. Word length for various columns is generally 1,000 words. Pays $100 to $300 on publication. Address column submissions to Attn: Associate Editor. For "Frontline" column, length limit is 350 to 400 words. Pays $50. Address to Attn: Frontline. Short stories should be between 1,500 and 3,000 words. Payment on individual basis. Address to Attn: Fiction Editor. All submissions must be typed. Include SASE for return of material. Send SASE for detailed guidelines. Sample copy for $2.50 plus 65¢ for postage and handling.

Editor's Remarks: "Our student interns do the majority of the writing. We seek intelligent, student-written pieces that fit our usual editorial format. Material from non-students will be considered. All submissions should appeal to males and females, particularly older teenagers. Articles should never talk down to readers, but still be lively, informative, interesting. If the manuscript is neatly typed, grammatically correct and contains no spelling errors, it is guaranteed to be read with a more sympathetic eye than a sloppy or shoddy submission. We *strongly* urge anyone wanting to submit material to read the magazine carefully. We receive hundreds of manuscripts that have no place in *Teenage,* however well-written."

Subscription Rates: One year in U.S. $17.95; in Canada $20.95; foreign $24.95. Write: *TeenAge,* P.O. Box 641, Holmes, PA 19043.

* TEENS TODAY, 6401 The Paseo, Kansas City, MO 64131. Weekly leisure-reading periodical for junior and senior high students; published by the Department of Youth of the Church of the Nazarene.

Publishes: Articles which speak to junior and senior high school students about their spiritual life and needs. Buys one fiction story per issue. Also buys some photos.

Subscription Info: Fiction should be between 1,200–1,500 words in length. Payment for accepted freelance articles is 3½¢ per word for first rights; 3¢ per word for reprint rights. Free sample copy and writer's guidelines available for SASE.

Editor's Remarks: "We are especially interested in articles which focus on holiness in the Wesleyan-Arminiam tradition. Here are some sample themes which *Teens Today* has addressed and to which we have committed ourselves in the future: self-appreciation, beginnings in Christ, discipleship, devotion, family and home, worship, sharing the Faith, spiritual freedom, world hunger, education, dealing with struggle/failure, future ambitions, friendship and dating, Christ's second coming, gifts/fruits of the Spirit, Christian fellowship, stewardship, giving in faith."

TEN PENNY PLAYERS, INC., 799 Greenwich St., New York, NY 10014.

Publishes: Books for and by children; material is developed through workshops and is not solicited.

Subscription Info: Write in c/o Barbara Fisher to above address for more complete information.

* THUMBPRINTS, 215 Ellington St., Caro, MI 48723. Monthly newsletter published by the Thumb Area Writer's Club.

Publishes: Various types of material including poetry, short fiction, articles, essays, information, how-to, opinions, etc. Accepts general topic information but prefers manuscripts which relate to writing, publishing or the writer's way of life. Also interested in short profiles. Will consider line drawings done in black ink. No photos.

Subscription Info: Material must be typed folowing standard formats. Will consider handwritten material only from writers 12 and under. Send SASE for possible return of manuscript. Stories and articles should be limited to 1,000 words. Prefers items of 500 words or less. Poems should not be longer than 32 lines. Pays in contributor's copies. Sample issue 50¢ each. You do not need to live in Michigan to submit material; however the work of club members and subscribers will be given first consideration. Send for yearly theme list for ideas.

Editor's Remarks: "We are always looking for manuscripts that inform or warm the hearts of amateur and professional writers alike. You do not need to be a member to submit material."

Subscription Rates: One year for non-member $8.50.

TROUVERE'S LAUREATE, Trouvere Company, Rt. 2, Box 290, Eclectic, AL 36024. Published tri-annually with poetry theme.

Publishes: Poetry, any style, length, or subject. Pays 15¢–25¢ per line. Illustrations, cartoons should be related to writing. Payment varies. Photographs should be accompanied by poem and related in theme. Pays $3 for photos. Enclose SASE for return of material. Writer's guidelines available for SASE.

Subscription Info: One year (three issues: spring, summer, fall-winter) $12. Random sample copy $2.50. Single current issue $4.00. Contributor's copies $3.50.

* TURTLE MAGAZINE FOR PRESCHOOL KIDS, 1100 Waterway Blvd., P.O. Box 567, Indianapolis, IN 46206. Monthly publication for children ages 2 to 5 from the Children's Better Health Institute. Stresses health-related themes or ideas including nutrition, safety, exercise, or proper health habits.

Publishes: From readers: artwork or pictures drawn or colored by the readers themselves.

Subscription Info: No payment is made for published reader material. All contributors may purchase copies in which their work appears at a reduced rate. Sample copies available for 75¢. Submissions should be limited to children ages 2–5.

Editor's Remarks: "Unfortunately, because of the many thousands of contributions we receive, we are not able to publish everything sent in to us."

Subscription Rates: One year $11.95. Special rate of $9.97 is usually offered in every issue.

* WATERWAYS: Poetry in the Mainstream, 799 Greenwich St., New York, NY 10014. Publication for audiences of children through adult.

Publishes: Poetry. No haiku and rarely uses rhyme. Does not use photographs but does use line drawings from contributors sometimes; primarily uses 19th century art. Although we prefer submissions to be typed, we read handwritten material as long as it is clear and in ink. We will send theme sheets to potential contributors if SASE accompanies the request. Pays in contributor's copy. Send SASE with all submissions. Address submissions to Barbara Fisher. Sample copy $2 plus 56¢ postage.

Editor's Remarks: "We receive submissions from all over the country and are interested to know a writer's school, if in school, and grade. Personal photos are not necessary."

Subscription Rates: For eleven issues $20.

†* WOMBAT: A Journal of Young People's Writing and Art, P.O. Box 8088, Athens, GA 30603. Publication which is comprised of creative work by young people ages 6 to 16.

Publishes: Poetry, short stories, artwork of all kinds, non-fiction articles, cartoons, etc. from young people ages 6 to 16.

Subscription Info: Material should include name, age, school address and home address of young person. Photo and brief autobiography for potential use on the "Contributor's" page may be included but is optional. Artwork, illustrations, picture stories must be originals or exceptionally clear copies of originals. Only artwork will be returned if accompanied by appropriately-sized SASE. Retain copies of written works or send legible, clear copies. (Also accepts Guest Adult Articles from professionals in any field on topics of interest to young people.) Young people whose work is accepted will receive a framable certificate and copy of the issue in which their work appears. If possible, a local newspaper will be notified of the event. Send SASE for guidelines. Sample copies $2.50.

Editor's Remarks: "*Wombat* is a comic-book size, easy to hold (and to tuck into a back pocket) publication, columned and printed in a typesize comfortable for young eyes to read, manage and enjoy. We hope our enthusiasm about being named a National PTA arts resource is contagious and that many people across the country will read this and will become interested enough to subscribe and, consequently, help us continue to 'be here' for our young people for a long time to come."

Subscription Rates: One year (eight issues) $14.95 for 1–5 subscriptions shipped to one address. Other bulk rate subscriptions available. Single copies $2.50.

* $ WORDWORKS, Young Writers' Newsletter, P.O. Box 216, Newburyport, MA 01950. For young writers ages 8 to 14.

Publishes: Only Young Writers' Club members may submit material. Once a member, you may submit as many manuscripts as you wish on poetry, short stories, fiction, non-fiction, letters, and word puzzles. Every subscriber automatically becomes a member. Does not use art from members.

Subscription Info: Each new member receives a note explaining submission requirements. Though *Wordworks* retains all rights, young writers may submit material elsewhere with no further permission needed. Material returned if accompanied by SASE. Reports immediately on submissions.

Editor's Remarks: "We love to publish as many submissions as we can for it is in the publication of young writers' work that young writers are encouraged. Because of limited space in the newsletter, we cannot print work from non-members. Neatness is crucial. We love personal information but only use name and age."

Subscription Rates: One year (ten issues) $11.95. Includes membership in the Young Writers' Club.

* WRITE TO FAME, P.O. Box 248, Youngtown, AZ 85363–0248. Monthly newsletter especially for writers ages 8 to 20 published by Keith Publications.

Publishes: Inspirational articles, contest and market news, plus poetry, short stories, and cartoons from writers ages 8 to 20.

Subscription Info: Short stories have 1,500 word limit. Uses poetry of all forms; cartoons dealing with writing, but will consider others. Also material for various columns including: Pen Pals, Fame News (a space to share good news), Why I Write (300 words or less), and others. Use standard formats. Send #10 SASE for detailed guidelines. Sample copy $1 plus #10 SASE.

Editor's Remarks: "Most articles are open to experienced freelancers but if a young writer has been published and can write an informative article to help other young writers it will be considered. My motto is 'Dream of your tomorrows and write your yesterdays today.' I encourage all young writers to write, but to suceed . . . you must submit!"

Subscription Rates: One year (12 issues) $12.

WRITER'S GAZETTE, Trouvere Company, Rt. 2., Box 290, Eclectic, AL 36024. Quarterly publication about, for, and by writers.

Publishes: Articles about writing. Maximum length 1,500 words. Short stories, any subject. Maximum length 2,500 words. Poetry, any subject, style, or length. Puzzles and quizzes related to writing, any style, and illustrations and cartoons related to writing. Payment varies. Other columns: *Chatty Patty's News & Notes*; book reports about new and old books (will also list self-published and trade published books); *Advice From Your Peers* (one goal of WG is not to *edit* manuscripts, therefore we encourage constructive criticism from our readers). Normally buys first time rights; will also consider previously published work. Send SASE for guidelines.

Subscription Rates: One year (four quarters: spring, summer, fall, winter) $18. Contributor's sample copy $4.

* WRITER'S INFO, P.O. Box 1870, Hayden, ID 83835. Published monthly, aimed toward beginning and intermediate writers and poets.

Publishes: Short poems and articles about writing.

Subscription Info: Poems should not be longer than 16 lines. Articles can be up to 300 words. Reports in one month, one-time rights used. Pays $1–$10 for first rights; payment in copies for previously published material. Sample copy and guidelines are free with SASE with two first class stamps.

Subscription Rates: One year $12.

* WRITERS NEWSLETTER, 1530 7th Street, Rock Island, IL 61201.

Publishes: News of interest to writers, how-to and inspirational pieces, and articles of interest to writers, short stories, vignettes and poems.

Subscription Info: Articles should be approximately 200 words. Short stories or vignettes should be limited to approximately 500 words. Poems, any style and subject, may not exceed 30 lines. Enclose SASE. Deadlines for newsletter submissions are: Dec. 1; Feb. 1; April 1; June 1; and August 1.

Subscription Rates: One year (6 issues) is $3.

* $ WRITER'S RESCUE, P.O. Box 248, Youngtown, AZ 85363–0248. Monthly newsletter for writers published by Keith Publications.

Publishes: Articles, poetry, markets, contests, challenges, inspirations, book reviews, special events, ideas, news from authors, editors, publishers and humorous stories about the life of writers.

Subscription Info: Use standard formats. Sample copy $1.50 plus #10 SASE. Send SASE for guidelines.

Editor's Remarks: "You must be a subscriber of one of our newsletters: *Writer's Rescue, Write to Fame,* or *Contests & Contacts.* If you are not and we decide to publish material you send, we'll *make* you a subscriber by subtracting the full magazine subscription cost from the price we'd pay for the article. Which newsletter is your choice. Submit as often as you like. If you've been published by us more than once, we'll note it with your article. Young writers will have their material published without pay if not a subscriber, but will receive a contributor's copy."

Subscription Rates: One year (12 issues) $12.

* WRITING!, c/o General Learning Corp., 60 Revere Dr., Northbrook, IL 60062–1563. Educational magazine for students in grades 7 to 12 published monthly during school year covering many aspects of writing (how-to, author profiles, etc.) with follow-up ideas for students to try.

Publishes: No fiction is accepted from anyone other than students. Does not accept other unsolicited manuscripts—prefers to see a query first. Each issue contains a "Student Writing" piece featuring a student-written manuscript (fiction, nonfiction, poetry, etc.). Also accepts questions about writing submitted by students. Each month, one question is chosen and a guest columnist prepares a response. Columnists include pulished writers, language experts, educators and professional journalists. Any query related to the process of writing (mechanics, usage, style, etc.) will be considered.

Subscription Info: Use standard format. Editors choose one piece of student writing on the basis of quality and reasonable length. Prefers manuscripts under 1,500 words. Students whose questions appear will be awarded $25. Sample copies are available.

Subscription Rates: Minimum 15 subscriptions to one address, $4.95 per student per school year; in Canada, $5.45 per student per school year.

* YOUNG JUDEAN, 50 West 58th St., New York, NY 10019. Publication of the Young Judean Zionist youth movement geared to 9–12 year olds, especially movement members.

Publishes: Material of Jewish interest only, emphasizing Israel, Jewish life and culture, holidays, religious tradition, Young Judean news and events, etc. Buys non-fiction, fiction, photos and fillers.

Subscription Info: Non-fiction articles: informational (300–1,000 words); how-to (300–500 words); personal experience, interviews, and personality profiles, historical pieces, opinion, travel (500–1,000 words); also reviews of books, movies, and Israeli records (300–800 words). Articles must be lively, preferably anecdotal, and appeal to a child's interests and point of view. Fiction of Jewish interest for children in all genres (500–1,500 words). Pays $20–$40 per story plus contributor's copies. Photos purchased with accompanying manuscript, 5 x 7″ maximum, captions requested. All forms of poetry accepted but must pertain to the Jewish and Zionist emphasis of the magazine. Puzzles, riddles, jokes, short humor—all with a Jewish slant—welcomed for fillers. Pays $5–$10 per poems, $5 a piece for fillers, plus contributor's copies. Sample copy available for 75¢. Guidelines for SASE.

Editor's Remarks: "Published by Hadassah Zionist Youth Commission, seven issues a year between September and June."

* YOUTH!, P.O. Box 801, Nashville, TN 37202. Published monthly by the United Methodist Publishing House for junior and senior high youth ages 13 to 18.

Publishes: Freelance fiction including adventure, romance, science fiction, fantasy, relationship stories, and humor which relate to and include one or more of the following: real human emotion and struggle, Christian identity, stories for *all* times and stories for *our* time, and creativity. Needs some stories aimed at junior high, some more suitable for senior high. Freelance articles should relate to or include one or more of the following: Christian identity, interesting topics (Does the subject matter interest today's teenagers?), a focus on the individual, real youth and situations. Uses a variety of writing styles. Uses quality photos for some articles.

Subscription Info: Both fiction and articles should be between 700-2,000 words in length. Double space, prefers lines of 53 typed characters. Include copies of reference and source identification if applicable. Include suggested subheads or blurbs and breaks in the story. In fiction avoid sex-role and racial sterotypes; avoid teenage stereotypes of the "Pretty People"—jocks, student body presidents, homecoming queens and stories that focus on them. Pays 4¢ per word for first-time serial rights. Detailed guidelines for both fiction, articles and for photos available for SASE. Model release forms needed from all recognizable people in submitted photos and slides.

Editor's Remarks: "The purpose of *Youth!* is to help teenagers live out the Christian faith in contemporary culture. We often get stories about death, but few fables, fantasies, or humor stories. We are delighted when we discover a surprise twist, a lovable and laughable character, a simple clever use of words, or a real faith experience. We treasure creativity in use of words, story line and format (writing style)."

Subscription Rates: One year $15.

CHAPTER SEVEN

Understanding a Contest Listing

There are many different types of contests listed in this Guide. Some are sponsored through various publishers, some by individual writing groups, and others by companies and associations. A few contests for photography and art have been included, usually when the entry requires a written caption or accompanying essay.

Each listing contains three individual sections of information which will help you understand (1) general information about the contest and its sponsor, (2) how entering the contest might benefit you, and (3) prize listings. There are also two optional sections. "Sponsor's Remarks" provides extra insight into the history or goals of the contest and/or advice for producing a winning entry. "Subscription Rates" has been included as an extra service for those interested in receiving a sponsor's publication on a regular basis.

New additions to this year's contest listings are preceded with a dagger (†). Contests which are of special interest to young people are preceded with an asterisk (*). Contests which require an entry fee are marked with a dollar sign ($).

Information for each listing was provided directly from the contest sponsor and is as current as possible. Be sure to send for a complete list of current rules and requirements for each contest you wish to enter.

The following chart and sample contest listing will help explain the information contained within each section.

CONTEST LISTING CHART

SECTION	YOU WILL FIND	PAY SPECIAL ATTENTION TO
1	Name of Contest Mailing address for entries, forms, and complete list of rules. Brief description including who is eligible, frequency of contest. Name of sponsor.	Who sponsors this contest and the general theme of each contest. The goal of the contest.
2	General information about the contest. Deadlines for entries. Eligibility requirements. Entry fees if any. How the contest will be judged. Avalability of rules and samples.	Any contests designed specifically for young people. Note any age limits. How to enter. Any restrictions.
3	Prizes awarded including cash, certificates, merchandise, and publication of winning entries.	The number of prizes awarded. How entries may be published. How often and how many times you may enter.
4	History of the contest, plus advice and tips for entering and winning quoted directly from the sponsor or entry form.	Advice to help you submit a winning entry.
5	Subscription rates if sponsored by a publication. Subscription mailing address when it differs from contest entry address.	Included as an extra service for young writers, parents, and teachers.

SAMPLE CONTEST LISTING

1 ———— **SHOE TREE CONTESTS FOR YOUNG WRITERS,** sponsored by the National Association for Young Writers, P.O. Box 452, Belvidere, NJ 07823. Writing contests for students ages 6 to 14.

2 ———— **General Info:** Each issue sponsors a different competition in one of three categories: fiction, non-fiction, and poetry. The contests are open to all children within age range and in first grade through eighth at time of entry. All work must be original and cannot have been previously published. A statement of authenticity signed by the student and by a parent, teacher, or guardian must accompany the entry. Students may submit no more than one entry for each category. Foreign language entries welcomed if accompanied by a translation. Stories may be illustrated. Student's name, address, age, the names of his or her school and teacher must accompany the entry. Submissions should be neatly written or typed. All entries become the property of the National Association for Young Writers. Entries must be postmarked no later than January 1st (fiction); April 1st (poetry); and June 1st (non-fiction). Send SASE for complete rules.

3 ———— **Prizes:** First prize in each of the categories is $25. Second prize in each category is $10. The winning entries, and those given honorable mention, will be published in *Shoe Tree.*

4 ———— **Sponsor's Remarks:** "We look for freshness and originality in the work of our prize winners. Formula stories and obvious "classroom" assignments are discouraged. Prize winners will be selected by *Shoe Tree*'s editorial staff."

5 ———— **Subscription Rates:** Send SASE to above address for current subscription rates for *Shoe Tree* and membership information in the NAYW.

CHAPTER EIGHT

The Contest List

†*$ **AGORA WRITING COMPETITIONS**, AG Publications, P.O. Box 10975, Raleigh, NC 27605. Sponsored through *Agora, The Magazine for Gifted Students* which is aimed at gifted secondary school students.

General Info: Entrants must subscribe or attend a school which subscribes to a class set of *Agora*. Contest categories include: short story, poetry, drama (one-act), public issues essay, literary analysis, scientific essay. Two divisions: Grades 7–9; Grades 10–12. Submission fee is $1.

Prizes: Cash prizes awarded plus possible publication in a nationally circulated magazine for secondary school students.

Sponsor's Remarks: "We are in our second year (1987) and have had only a small number of entries thus far."

Subscription Rates: One year (4 issues during school year) $9 for individuals; $7.50 per student in class set (20 or more to one address); $20 for teacher's supplement.

* **AMERICA & ME ESSAY CONTEST**, Farm Bureau Insurance Group, Communications Dept., 7373 W. Saginaw, Lansing, MI 48909. Yearly contest which encourages Michigan young people to explore their roles in America's future.

General Info: Open to any eighth grade student in any school in

Michigan. Students must participate through their school systems. Interested students and schools should contact the main office or a Farm Bureau insurance agent in their area for complete information and requirements. Each school may submit up to 10 essays for judging. A first, second, and third place winner will be selected from each school. Each first place essay is automatically entered into the state-wide competition from which the top essays are selected. Essays must relate to yearly theme and may be up to 500 words long. (Topic examples: 1986–87 "How I Can Contribute to America's Future"; 1987–88 "What the Future of America Holds for Me"). Schools must preregister their intended involvement.

Prizes: First through third place winners in each school receive certificate. First place winner's name also appears on plaque that hangs permanently in his or her school. The top ten state-wide winners each receive a plaque plus they share $5,500 in savings bonds ranging from $1,000 for first place to $500 for tenth place. In addition, the top ten essays plus selected excerpts from other essays are compiled into a booklet and distributed to schools, government leaders and the general public.

Sponsor's Remarks: "This (1987–88) is the contest's 19th year. Since it was started in 1968, more than 110,000 students have participated. Average participation each year is now over 10,000 students. The final ranking of the top 10 winners is made by a panel of VIP judges that in the past has included Governors Blanchard and Milliken and former President Gerald Ford. Hundreds of newspapers print stories about local winners and may also reprint essays of winners on the school level providing additional recognition for the students. As sponsor of the contest, Farm Bureau has earned 11 national awards from the Freedoms Foundation at Valley Forge."

Subscription Rates: Sample of the compiled essays are available through Farm Bureau at the above address.

* AMERICAN LEGION NATIONAL HIGH SCHOOL ORATORICAL CONTEST, The American Legion, P.O. Box 1055, Indianapolis, IN 46206. Nationally sponsored speech contest whose purpose is to develop a deeper knowledge and appreciation of the Constitution of the United States on the part of high school students.

General Info: The subject used must be on some phase of the Constitution which will give emphasis to the attendant duties and obligations of a citizen to our government. Prepared oration must be the original effort of each contestant and must not take up less than eight minutes or more than ten minutes for delivery. Eligible participants must be citizens of the United States. All contestants must be bona fide students herein described as any student under the age of 20 years on the date of the National Finals Contest who is presently enrolled in a high school or junior high school in which the curriculum is considered to be of high school level. Contact local American Legion Post or write to above address for complete brochure.

Prizes: Four finalists receive scholarships from the National Organization of The American Legion which may be used to attend any college or university in the United States. Scholarship amounts are: winner, $16,000; runner-up, $14,000; third place, $10,000; fourth place, $8,000. Each Legion Department (State) winner who participates in the contest at the regional level receives a $1,000 scholarship. Each Sectional participant who does not advance to the National Finals receives an additional $1,000 scholarship.

Sponsor's Remarks: "In its 51st year, the contest was among the first activities "officially recognized" by the Federal Commission on the Bicentennial of the U.S. Constitution. The contest was cited as a program with 'exceptional merit' by the Commission. Since the program's inception, The American Legion has awarded over $1.2 million in college scholarships. Additional awards are presented at the Legion Department (State) level. Contest conducted in all 50 states in addition to the District of Columbia, Puerto Rico, Mexico and France."

*$ AMHA ART CONTEST, American Morgan Horse Association, P.O. Box 1, Westmoreland, NY 13490. Annual art contest open to both professional and amateur artists.

General Info: The competition is divided into two design categories: Morgan art and Morgan cartoons. Morgan art could include such art forms as pencil sketches, watercolors, oils, sculptures, etc. Artists may enter as many works as they wish. A $1 entry fee and entry form are required for each work. Write to the above address for complete information and entry forms.

Prizes: Both professionals and amateurs will be competing in the following categories: (1) 13 and under; (2) 14–21; (3) adult. Cash awards will be given to five places in each category and division as follows: first $60, second $45, third $30, fourth $20, fifth $10. Ribbons will be given to ten places in each category and division. The winning art works and others selected will be exhibited at the AMHA Convention and will appear in *The Morgan Horse* magazine.

*$ AMHA PHOTO CONTEST, American Morgan Horse Association, P.O. Box 1, Westmoreland, NY 13490. Annual contest for both professional and amateur photographers. Yearly theme.

General Info: Photographs may be color or black and white prints, 5″ x 7″ or 8″ x 10″ in size. A $1 entry fee is required for each photo. You may enter as many photos as you wish. A separate entry form should be used for each photo submitted. Photos will be judged on creativity, spontaneity of subject, technical quality, breed promotion and overall appearance. Deadline is December 1 for 1988 and 1989. Write to the above address for complete information and copy of entry form.

Prizes: Ribbons and cash awards will be given to ten places: first $150, second $125, third $100, fourth $75, fifth $50, and sixth through tenth $25.

* ARIZONA STATE POETRY SOCIETY ANNUAL CONTEST, c/o Jack Evans, 7722 W. Devonshire Ave., Phoenix, AZ 85033. Annual poetry contest open to all poets regardless of age or location featuring 12 individual categories. Also a special contest for high school students from Arizona.

General Info: Regular contests open to all poets regardless of location. High School contest *only* open to Arizona high school students grades 9–12. Only unpublished poems, not under consideration elsewhere prior to announced awards may be entered. No duplicate entries. Published poems awarded less than $10 monetary value may be entered. Poems may be in any form, 40 line limit. No entry fee required for high school contest. Entry fees of $1 or $2 on open contests. Send SASE for complete rules and entry format required for all sponsored categories.

Prizes: Winning poems for all contests (including high school) will be published in ASPS Quarterly, *The Sandcutters.* A complimentary copy is given to cash winners. Cash prizes for student winners are $75, $50 and $25. All winners receive certificates. All honorable mentions will be listed in publication. Poems not placing will be destroyed.

Sponsor's Remarks: "ASPS has been in existance for 21 years and we have held contests for 20 years. We have over 3,000 entrants a year now and offer over $900 in cash prizes. For ASPS, the contest provides us with an opportunity to promote quality poetry and to give poets a place to have their work recognized."

Subscription Rates: Send SASE for subscription information.

* $ ARTS RECOGNITION AND TALENT SEARCH, National Foundation for Advancement of the Arts, 100 North Biscayne Blvd., Miami, FL 33132. Scholarship opportunities for high school students interested in dance, music, theatre, visual arts and writing.

General Info: Contact your teacher, guidance counselor or principal for complete registration packet. ARTS program is designed for high school seniors and other 17–18 year olds with demonstrable artistic achievements in dance, music, theater, visual arts (including film and video) and writing. Application materials will also be sent to individuals by request. Fee of $25 for each discipline or discipline category entered; more for late entry.

Prizes: NFAA earmarks up to $400,000 in cash awards for ARTS applicants whose work has been judged as outstanding by a national panel of experts. Selected candidates are also invited to Miami, Florida for a week of live adjudications, consisting of auditions, master and technique classes, workshops, studio exercises and interviews. NFAA pays travel, lodging and meal expenses for the cash award candidates. Additional college scholarships and internships, worth over $3,000,000, have also been made available to all ARTS participants whether or not they were award winners.

Sponsor's Remarks: "ARTS is a unique program in that applicants are judged against a standard of excellence within each art discipline, *not* against each other. ARTS does not pre-determine the number of awards to be made on any level or in any discipline."

* AVON/FLARE NOVEL COMPETITION, Avon Books, 105 Madison Ave., New York, NY 10016. Biannual contest for writers ages 13 to 18.

General Info: Each manuscript should be approximately 125 to 200 pages, or about 30,000 to 50,000 words based on 250 words per page. Manuscript must be written by a teen (ages 13 to 18) and be about teenagers and for teenagers. All manuscripts must follow standard format. Along with manuscript enclose a letter that includes a short description of your novel, your name, address, telephone number and age. Enclose both SASE for return of manuscript and SAS postcard to acknowledge receipt of your manuscript. Be sure to keep a copy of your manuscript. Send for poster containing complete information.

Prizes: Winner receives $2,500 advance against royalties and a publishing contract.

Sponsor's Remarks: "This is a biannual contest occurring in odd numbered years. The 1987 contest is the third time this contest has been held. Avon usually receives approximately 500 entries. We're looking for young writers who show narrative talent and writing ability. The winning manuscript will be chosen for these qualities."

†*$ BIG APPLE AWARDS, *The Apple Blossom Connection*, c/o Mary M. Blake, Editor, P.O. Box 325, Stacyville, IA 50476. Offers award six times per year.

General Info: Contests held six times each year for best poetry (maximum 36 lines); fiction (maximum 1,500 words); non-fiction (1,000); or drama (one-act plays only). Use standard formats. Enter any number of original, unpublished manuscripts during any time period. Your name, address, and "The Big Apple Competition" must appear at the top of your manuscript. Send $2 entry fee for each manuscript entered; $1 fee for subscribers. Make checks payable to: Peak Output. Manuscripts judged on format, content and style. Write with

SASE for detailed guidelines and deadlines.

Prizes: Guaranteed prize of $25 for best fiction, non-fiction or drama manuscript received during qualifying time period. Guaranteed prize of $5 awarded for best poetry manuscript. Prizes are not dependent on the number of entries received. Winners will also receive certificate and publication of the winning manuscript in The Apple Blossom Connection.

Sponsor's Remarks: "We began publishing in May of 1987. Our first "Big Apple" awards were given in October, 1987. Because we are a small press just beginning, entrants have a better chance to win since contest is not large yet."

Subscription Rates: One year $10. Two years $18. Make checks payable to Peak Output.

BITTERROOT POETRY CONTESTS, *Bitterroot,* Editor: Menke Katz, Box 489, Spring Glen, NY 12483-0489. Sponsors two annual poetry contests.

General Info: Send SASE for complete rules for: William Kushner Annual Awards and Heershe David-Badonneh Award. Contestants need not be subscribers. Poems should not exceed 30 lines. No more than 3 poems may be entered. Each poem must be original and unpublished, typed on a separate page which includes author's name, address, and the contest in which the poem is entered on the upper left-hand corner of the reverse side of the page. Use *only* letter size (#10) envelopes. If entering more than one contest, please submit in separate envelopes. Deadline for either contest is December 31.

Prizes: For William Kushner Award: first place $60; second place $40; third place $25. For Heershe David-Badonneh Award: first place $100; second place $60; third place $40.

Sponsor's Remarks: "We seek to inspire and encourage poets."

Subscription Rates: To *Bitterroot Poetry Magazine*: One year (3 issues April, August, December) $10. Two years $18. Three years $25.

* $ BYLINE STUDENT CONTESTS, P.O. Box 130596, Edmond,

OK 73013. Special contests for students during school year sponsored by *Byline* magazine which is aimed at beginning writers.

General Info: Variety of monthly writing contests for students 18 years and younger beginning with September issue and continuing through May each year. Prefers typewritten entries on white bond paper 8″ x 11″. Most contests have small entry fee which provides cash awards to winners. Other categories have no entry fee and are often used as class assignments by writing and English teachers. Send SASE for details of upcoming contests. Sample copy $3.

Prizes: Cash prizes and possible publication of students' manuscripts.

Sponsor's Remarks: "*Byline* contests provide motivation for young writers who enjoy winning cash awards, seeing their names and writing in print and meeting deadlines."

Subscription Rates: One year (12 issues) $18.

$ CALIFORNIA STATE POETRY SOCIETY MONTHLY CONTESTS, c/o Selma D. Calnan, 363 S. 5th Ave, La Puente, CA 91746. Sponsors a wide variety of contests during the year.

General Info: Open to any and all poets. Contest themes vary from month to month. Send SASE to receive current list of themes, complete information and deadlines. Any number of poems may be submitted in any contest; however, do not combine poems in one envelope intended for more than one contest. Fees for each month's contest vary according to number of poems entered. Examples of themes: narrative poems; poems on a dream; fantasy or illusion; your most tender poems; light or humorous poem about an animal; any subject, any form. Poems must be original, unpublished work of the poet; must not be submitted to other contest or publisher until one month after contest deadline, and shall not have received a prize of over $5 (except December contest for previously published poems). Poems must be clearly typed or duplicated on 8″ x 11″ white paper. Include SASE with all submissions.

Prizes: There will be one prize for each monthly contest consisting of one-half the total entry fees. One winner and two runners-up will be notified within the contest month, and announced in a CSPS

Newsletter. No poems will be published by CSPS.

Sponsor's Remarks: "All poems remain the property of their authors, and may be submitted elsewhere one month after contest deadline."

†* CANADIAN AUTHOR & BOOKMAN ANNUAL CREATIVE WRITING CONTEST, *Canadian Author & Bookman Magazine,* 121 Avenue Rd., Suite 104, Toronto, Ontario M5R 2G3. For students enrolled in Canadian secondary and post-secondary schools.

General Info: Categories include poetry, fiction and non-fiction. All entries *must* be accompanied by an official entry form, clipped from a copy of *Canadian Author & Bookman.* Additional copies of entries available from the above address. No photocopies or other copies are permitted. Each student may enter only once in each category, and each teacher may sponsor only one student per category. Fiction and non-fiction entries may not exceed 2,500 words in length. Poetry entries may not exceed 50 lines. All entries must be original, unpublished, and not submitted to any other national contest. Use standard format but *do not* put any identification mark on manuscript other than the title. See official entry form for further information, complete rules and current deadlines.

Prizes: One prize of $100 is offered in each category, with a matching award going to the teacher who sponsors the winner. In addition, a $500 scholarship is available to the student who, in the opinion of the judges, shows the most promise, regardless of that student's final standing in the contest. This student, when chosen, must provide certification of college enrollment.

Sponsor's Remarks: "The contest is sponsored by the Canadian Authors Association. Its aim is to encourage student writing at the secondary and post-secondary levels in Canada. The 1988 contest is our Fifth Annual Contest."

† COMMUNITY CHILDREN'S THEATRE ANNUAL PLAY-WRITING CONTEST, sponsored by the Community Children's Theatre of Kansas City, Inc. Address entries to: Mrs. Blanche Sellens, 8021 East 129th Terrace, Grandview, MO 64030. Provides live theatre for elementary aged children in 250 elementary schools yearly using 6 trouping units which are composed of women volunteers.

General Info: Over the past 34 years, 50 original scripts resulting from this contest have been produced by the theatre's trouping units. Plays must be written for elementary school age audience. Plays should have eight or fewer characters. All characters are performed by women; therefore, male roles should not be overly virile. The location is different for each presentation; therefore, technical requirements must take this into account. Manuscripts should be typed, double-spaced and securely bound. Author's name and address must appear on the fly-page. Published plays are not acceptable. Do not submit seasonal plays as productions are trouped throughout the school year. Write to the above address for complete contest rules, requirements and deadlines.

Prizes: An award of $500 will be given for the best script submitted. In the event that two or more scripts are judged worthy of the award, the prize money will be apportioned at the discretion of the Reading Committee. Winners will be announced in April, and the award made in May. Community Children's Theatre reserves the right for one of its troupes to produce any prize-winning play royalty-free whether it is produced one year or two consecutive years.

Sponsor's Remarks: "Although our 5 to 12-year-old audiences are sophisticated, gratuitious violence, mature love stories, or slang are not appropriate. Cursing is *not acceptable*. In addition to original ideas, subjects that usually provide good plays are: legends, folklore, historical incidents, biographies, and adaptations of children's classics."

* $ CONTESTS & CONTACTS, P.O. Box 248, Youngtown, AZ 85363–0248. Monthly contests sponsored by Keith Publications.

General Info: Send SASE for detailed list of monthly themes.

Prizes: First place $2 plus publication of entry.

Sponsor's Remarks: "We like to encourage young writers."

Subscription Rates: One year (12 issues) $18.

$ CREATIVE WITH WORDS ANNUAL POETRY CONTEST,
CWW, P.O. Box 223226, Carmel, CA 93922. For any age writer.

General Info: Sponsors one annual poetry contest, relating to various themes (1983 theme was "Mankind;" 1984 theme was "Animals"). Fee is $1 per poem entered. Enter as many poems as you wish; however, only one poem per poet can win a prize. There is a 10 line minimum, 20 line maximum, with no more than 42 characters across a line. Enclose one SASE and one SAS postcard with entry. Send SASE for current contest rules and deadlines.

Prizes: First place and down receive $15, $10, $5, $1.

Sponsor's Remarks: "Nineteen eight-five annual poetry contest held in celebration of CWW's 10th anniversary."

* CRICKET LEAGUE CONTESTS, *Cricket,* P.O. Box 300, Peru, IL 61354. Monthly contests for children ages 5 to 14 sponsored through *Cricket* magazine.

General Info: Contest themes vary from month to month. Refer to a current issue of magazine. Throughout the year, contests are sponsored in three categories: art, poetry, and short story. There are two age groups for each contest: 5–9 year olds and 10–14 year olds. All contest rules must be followed. Rules are listed in each issue. You must have your parent's or guardian's permission to send your entry. Each entry must be signed by your parent or guardian saying it is your own original work and that no help was given. If entry is typed, the original handwritten story or poem must be sent with the typed version. Deadlines are the 25th of each month.

Prizes: Winners receive prizes or certificates and most place-winners' entries are published in the magazine.

Sponsor's Remarks: " The *Cricket* League has sponsored contests since the magazine's inception in September of 1973. Through these contests, children have an opportunity to experience the rewards that creative writing and drawing bring."

Subscription Rates: Single copy $2. One year $22.50. Two years $39.70. Three years $58.

C.S.P. WORLD NEWS CONTESTS, Box 2608, Station D, Ottawa, Ontario, Canada, K1P 5W7. Contests sponsored by monthly publication stressing poetry. International readership.

General Info: Send IRC for complete information about upcoming contests. No restrictions.

Prizes: Publication of winning poems. Benefits include exposure of beginner's work.

Sponsor's Remarks: "The goal is to develop talent. *C.S.P. World News* is 23 years old (1988). In the January issue of each year, the whole list of winning poets is published, usually on the front page. Good company indeed."

† * **DADA SHORT STORY CONTEST**, Detroit Auto Dealers Association, 1800 W. Big Beaver Rd., Troy, MI 48084. Sponsored yearly by the Detroit Auto Dealers Association. Special division for high school students added in 1987.

General Info: Short story contest limited to Michigan schools only. Send SASE to Joann Meidl, assistant director Detroit Auto Show, for complete information of upcoming contest; ask whether special division for high school students is included.

Prizes: In 1987, high school contest winners were awarded $500 for first, $250 for second, and $100 for third. Winning stories are often published in special yearly Detroit Auto Show Program.

Sponsor's Remarks: "We would like to see more participation, especially from high school students."

*$ **DOG WRITERS' ASSOCIATION OF AMERICA ANNUAL WRITING CONTESTS**, c/o M. Akers-Hanson, Box 301, Kewanee, IL 61443 (309) 856-7891. Various contest categories for writers of all ages. Also sponsors scholarship awards for young people through the Dog Writers' Educational Trust.

General Info: Entries must be published, dog-related material: articles, short stories, poetry, cartoons, books. Open to all writers. Entry fee $8. Entries must be postmarked by October 1 each year. Send SASE for current rules, complete list of categories, detailed submission guidelines, and official entry form. The Educational Trust is seeking young applicants who are desirous of becoming dog journalists, veterinarians, or who have given extensively to the sport of showing dogs through raising pure-bred dogs and participating in various junior showmanship activities. Applications can be obtained from: Mrs. Robert H. Futh, Jr., Kinney Hills Rd., Washington Depot, CT 06794.

Prizes: Include plaques and/or certificates and publicity in dog-oriented press; three $500 cash awards; one $200 cash award.

Sponsor's Remarks: "The field is wide open and eager for new writers and new perspectives. Go for it! Our faith in young people is exemplified through the scholarship awards by the Dog Writers' Educational Trust."

* ELIAS LIERBERMAN STUDENT POETRY AWARD, The Poetry Society of America, 15 Gramercy Park South, New York, NY 10003. One of many annual poetry contests sponsored annually by PSA.

General Info: Open to high school students (grades 9–12) from the U.S. and its territories. Poem must be previously unpublished. No line limit. Send for complete submission rules and requirements, as well as a list of all contests sponsored by PSA.

Prizes: For best poem $100.

† THE GROUP THEATRE'S MULTI-CULTURAL PLAY-WRIGHT'S FESTIVAL, The Group Theatre Company, 3940 Brooklyn Ave. N.E., Seattle, WA 98105. Annual contest.

General Info: Open to any playwright whose ethnic background is Black, Hispanic/Chicano, Asian, or Native American. Seeking previously unproduced one-act and full-length scripts. No musicals or children's plays. Send SASE for current deadline, announcement and festival schedule. Interested playwrights should send scripts, cover letter, resume and SASE to above address, Attn: Festival.

Prizes: Air fare, housing and an honorarium will be awarded to two winning playwrights. Their scripts will be given two weeks of workshop development and four performances during the Festival. Six other scripts will be given cold readings during the Festival.

* GUIDEPOSTS YOUTH WRITING CONTEST, 747 Third Avenue, New York, NY 10017. Sponsored annually by *Guideposts* magazine for high school juniors and seniors.

General Info: Open to any high school junior or senior, or students in equivalent grades in other countries. Send for complete rules. Entrants must write a first-person story telling about a true, personal experience of the writer. All manuscripts must be the original work of the student submitting the entry and must be written in English. Use standard format. Maximum limit of 1,200 words. Entries must include: home address, phone number, and name and address of entrant's school. Write for current deadlines. Winners will be notified by mail prior to announcement in *Guideposts*. Prize-winning manuscripts become the property of *Guideposts*. Send SASE for return of non-winning manuscripts.

Prizes: Authors of the top 10 manuscripts, as judged by the editors of *Guideposts*, will receive a scholarship and a portable electronic typewriter. Scholarships to the accredited colleges or schools of contest winners' choice will be in the following amounts: First prize $6,000; second $5,000; third $4,000; fourth $3,000; fifth $2,000; sixth through tenth $1,000; eleventh through thirtieth receive portable typewriters. Prizes are not redeemable in cash, not transferable and must be used within five years after high school graduation. All decisions of the judges are final.

Sponsor's Remarks: "A winning story doesn't have to be complicated or filled with drama. It only has to come from the heart, and be an honest and straightforward account of an experience that touched you deeply or changed your ideas or outlook. Think of something that happened to you at home, at school, or at a job: an exciting close call, or a tough personal decision that took moral courage. Then write about it as if you were telling a story to a friend. Don't be shy about revealing your own innermost feelings. Study *Guideposts* stories to see how others present their experiences. Then look at what's happened in your own life and do the same."

$ HAIKU AND CAPPING LINES CONTEST, *Dragonfly: East/West Quarterly,* Middlewood Press, P.O. Box 11236, Salt Lake City, UT 84118.

General Info: Quarterly haiku contest, and other haiku and linking verse contests, rules and topic are featured in each issue, but author must see the current issue to know subjects and rules. No more than four haiku may be entered, each haiku typed on one side of half of 8″ x 11″ paper. Entry fee per haiku is 25¢. Put name and address on back of each entry in upper left-hand corner. "Dragonfly Quarterly Contest" should be typed above haiku in upper right-hand corner. Include SASE with entries. The subject for haiku is whatever the current season is; that is, if the author is writing in summer, the haiku should reflect summer in some way. Free guidelines on haiku available. Sample copies are $3.50.

Prizes: For haiku contest, first prize is 50% of amount collected in entry fees; second and third prizes are 25% each of amount collected in entry fees. Winning poems, including runners-up, are published in *Dragonfly*. For capping lines contests, first, second, and third prizes are $5, $3, and $2.

Sponsor's Remarks: "The capping lines contest began in 1973 and has formed a continuous linked poem since then of over 50 links (stanzas). Every two years the poem is published in its entirety with the new winning capping lines added on. Since haiku and linked verse (also known as renga) are specialized forms of poetry, the poet is urged to buy at least one copy of the magazine and study it. We are close to our 70th quarterly haiku contest. The magazine has been in existence for sixteen years."

Subscription Rates: Sample copies for $3.50 each. In U.S. one year $12. In Canada $14.

† * **HENRY FONDA YOUNG PLAYWRIGHTS PROJECT**, Very Special Arts, Education Office, The John F. Kennedy Center for the Performing Arts, Washington, D.C. 20566. International organization dedicated to enriching the lives of children, youth and adults with disabilities; creates opportunities for disabled and non-disabled to celebrate and share accomplishments in drama, dance, music, literature, and the visual arts.

General Info: Plays written by students between the ages of 12 and 18 featuring some aspect of disability. Students may write from their own experience or about some experience in the life of other people. Students are encouraged to investigate the topic. Three typewritten copies of script must be sent. Also include the following information: author's name, date of birth, telephone number, and a short, biographical description of the author. If there is more than one author per script, include full information for each. Write to above address to receive detailed brochure.

Prizes: The young playwright whose work is chosen, and a chaperone, will travel to Washington, D.C. at the expense of Very Special Arts to participate in rehearsals and be an honored guest at the premiere production. If finalist script is written by multiple authors, VSA will assist with financial support for the trip.

Sponsor's Remarks: "Although the play must address or otherwise incorporate some aspect of disability, the choice of theme, setting and style is up to you. Sometimes people who aren't familiar with the theatre want to first try playwriting with friends. If working in a group would help you, that's fine with us, as long as all the playwrights are between the ages of twelve and eighteen."

* IN TOUCH ANNUAL WRITING CONTEST, Box 50434, Indianapolis, IN 46250. For young adults ages 13 to 19 as of November 1st of the current year. Sponsored by *In Touch* magazine.

General Info: Entrants must be at least 13 and no older than 19 as of the deadline date (usually November). Write a true or fictional article showing how God works in the lives of teens. It could be a problem that taught you more about God; how God has worked in your youth group or in personal relationships; it can even be science fiction or fantasy that involves God and teens. All entries must be typed and not more than 1,500 words. Include name, address, home church, and age in the top left-hand corner of the first page. In top right-hand corner specify if it's fiction or a true story. Put name in top left-hand corner of each additional page. Send for current rules and complete information.

Prizes: Cash awards of $100, $75, $50 for first, second and third place entries respectively. Top three stories will also be printed in September issue.

Sponsor's Remarks: "Stories will be judged on the basis of clarity, style, word choice, relevance to *In Touch* readers and overall impact."

† **IUPUI NATIONAL CHILDREN'S THEATRE PLAYWRITING COMPETITION**, 525 N. Blackford St., Indianapolis, IN 46202. Biennial playwriting competition sponsored by Indiana University-Purdue University at Indianapolis (IUPUI).

General Info: Only original plays may be entered. May include music. If the play is an adaptation or dramatization of material, written proof must be provided that the original work is in the public domain or permission of the author is granted. Manuscripts must be typed and securely bound with the title clearly visible. Author's name should not appear on the bound manuscript. Submit three copies of the completed manuscript. Scripts must have 45 minutes minimum/75 minutes maximum running time; 6–12 in cast (may include doubling). Only scripts which have not been previously, professionally produced may be entered. Entry form must accompany each script. Send SASE for detailed guidelines and other information.

Prizes: First place: up to $1,500 (one-half to be used toward residency while winning play is produced.) Three runners-up: up to $500 each (to be used toward residency while play receives rehearsed reading.)

Sponsor's Remarks: "While the majority of the entrants for the past two competitions have been adults, we do not exclude young writers provided they meet the guidelines. We have held two biennial competitions and have received over 250 scripts from throughout the U.S. and Canada. The competition has as a companion activity a national symposium on children's theatre which features productions of the winning scripts and workshops helpful to playwrights and children's theatre professionals."

† * **JUNIOR EDITOR**, 709 S.E. 52nd Avenue, Ocala, FL 32671. Magazine featuring material written by studnets of all ages through high school.

General Info: Sponsors a variety of monthly contests on different topics. Contests are announced in each issue of *Junior Editor.*

Prizes: Prizes vary according to contest. See magazine for details.

Sponsor's Remarks: "We are especially looking for work from students in grades 5 through high school."

Subscription Rates: One year for teachers $10. One year for others $20.

$ JUST A LITTLE POEM, Trouvere Company, Rt. 2, Box 290, Eclectic, AL 36024. Tri-annual publication of a monthly contest.

General Info: Short poems only, 2–12 lines. Any style or subject. All poems must be previously unpublished. All entries should indicate the month they are submitted for. If not, they will be entered in the month they arrive. Limit of 5 poems per month. There is *no* fee to subscribers. For non-subscribers the fee is 50¢ per poem. Entries will not be returned. SASE must accompany each group of entries. Publication deadlines: June issue contains Feb., March, April, May. October issue contains June, July, Aug., Sept. February issue contains Oct., Nov., Dec., Jan. Send SASE for complete information.

Prizes: First place $20, plus 5 extra copies. Second place $5, plus 3 extra copies. Third place $3, plus 2 extra copies. Honorable mention will be given in each publication to those poems that did not win an award but still stood out from the rest.

Sponsor's Remarks: "We try to publish as many poems as we can from the contest, but we have limited space. Therefore, if your poem is not printed, you are welcome to enter it again as long as it adheres to the rest of the rules. After the winners are picked, we randomly pick other poems to publish. This gives entrants an opportunity to see what poems were submitted."

Subscription Rates: One year (3 issues) $5. Extra copies 50¢ each or 3/$1.00.

† * KENTUCKY STATE POETRY SOCIETY CONTESTS, c/o James W. Proctor, 505 Southland Blvd., Louisville, KY 40214. Variety of annual poetry contests for both students and adults.

General Info: One special category for elementary school students grades 1–3; one category for students grades 4–6; and one category for high school students grades 7–12. Also special category for college students, regardless of age. No entry fees for student categories; entry fees vary according to number of manuscripts entered. Poems must be the original work of the poet. Teacher or parent may *suggest* subject matter or advise as to poetry techniques only, and may stress adherence to rules, importance of correct spelling, grammar and punctuation, neatness and legibility. Student entries may be untyped, but copy must be neat and legible. No poem will be returned; keep your own copy. Do not submit poems currently submitted in another contest or for publication. Send SASE for list of current categories and specific details *each* year.

Prizes: Only first place winners will be published. Varying cash awards and certificates awarded.

Sponsor's Remarks: "This contest cannot be successfully entered without a new Contest Sheet each year, as the contests may not always be the same! Contest Chairman may change without notice and we cannot handle any entries without SASE."

Subscription Rates: For Prize Edition of *Pegasus*, send check for $3.50 by October 31. Order from: Ruth P. Clark, Route 3, Box 16, Old Boston Rd, Lebanon Junction, KY 40150. For other subscription requests, send SASE to same address.

* LISTEN, JOURNAL OF BETTER LIVING, 6830 Laurel Street NW, Washington, DC 20012.

General Info: Contests announced in *Listen* magazine.

Sponsor's Remarks: "We do not have contests annually; we have them sporadically. Had one in 1982 and one in 1985. When we have them, we have a section for unpublished authors though age is irrelevant."

* $ MISSISSIPPI VALLEY POETRY CONTEST, Box 3021, Davenport, IA 52808. Wide variety of poetry contests held annually for the past 14 years. Sponsored mainly by the Quad City Writers Club, Writer's Studio, and Contemporary Writers Roundtable, plus other various sponsors.

General Info: Of special interest to young writers is the Junior Division for best poem by a senior high school student, best poem by a junior high student, and best poem by an elementary school student. Other categories include: religious poems, historical, and rhyming. Conditions and restrictions are set forth in the rules which are updated annually. Final judges are selected persons from local educational institutions. Copy of current rules available for SASE. Entry fees are minimal; check current contest rules sheet.

Prizes: In Junior Division, each winning high school, junior high, and elementary school student receives $10. For other divisions, winners receive $25. Prizes may change; see current contest rules.

Sponsor's Remarks: "We endeavor to keep entry fees low for the benefit of students, senior citizens, and those hard pressed In the past, we have had entries from every state but the Dakotas. Why? Don't know."

NATIONAL PLAY AWARD, National Repertory Theatre Foundation, Box 71011, Los Angeles, CA 90071. Sponsors playwriting award for original plays.

General Info: Entries must be original plays conceived for production on the living stage; no musicals, translations, or adaptations. No entry forms are required, however, a brief biography of the author and a history of the play must be sumitted with the script. NRTF retains no rights and seeks no claims on plays submitted. Entries must not have been previously submitted to the National Play Award, published, produced on the professional stage (with a paid Equity cast), or have already won a major play award. Scripts must be submitted in a professional script format: in covers, typed, and legibly photocopied. Write NRTF for a fact sheet for current play award information including current deadlines.

Prizes: To the playwright, $7,500 cash award; and $5,000 to a qualified professional theatre to aid production of the winning script.

Sponsor's Remarks: "Entries will not be returned unless accompanied by SASE. Do not send checks, cash, or money orders to cover postage."

† $ THE NATIONAL POETRY SERIES, The Ecco Press, 26 West 17th St., New York, NY 10011. Annual open competition for books of poetry.

General Info: Competition open to American citizens only for book length (48–64 pages), typed manuscripts of poetry. All manuscripts must be previously unpublished, though some or all of the poems may have appeared in periodicals. Books previously self-published and chapbooks are not eligible. Entry fee of $15 must accompany manuscript. Send SASE for complete list of rules and current deadlines. Entries for 1988 competition end February 15, 1988.

Prizes: Five books of poetry will be chosen. Five predetermined publishers will each publish one of the books which will be added to, and promoted with, their regular list.

Sponsor's Remarks: "The National Poetry Series was established in 1978 to publish five books of poetry through participating publishers."

† * NATIONAL WRITTEN & ILLUSTRATED BY . . . AWARDS CONTEST FOR STUDENTS, by Landmark Editions, Inc., 1420 Kansas Ave., Kansas City, MO 64127. Annual book contest for students in three age categories.

General Info: Original books by students may be entered in three age categories: 6–9, 10–13, and 14–19 years of age. Text and pictures must be written and illustrated by students themselves. Send SASE for copy of complete contest rules and guidelines.

Prizes: Winners receive all-expense paid trip to Landmark's offices in Kansas City, where editors and art directors assist them in the final preparation of text and illustrations for the publication of their books. Winners also receive publishing contracts and are paid royalties.

Sponsor's Remarks: "Contest sponsored to encourage and celebrate the creativity of students. More than 1,600 original book entries came from every state in the Union and from Canada, too. The winning books were selected by a national panel of distinguished educators, editors, art directors, and 22 authors and illustrators of juvenile books."

* NFSPS STUDENT AWARD, National Federation of State Poetry Societies, Inc. *Strophes* Editor, Kay Kinnaman, 1121 Major Avenue NW, Albuquerque, NM 87107. Annual award for students in grades 6–12. Sponsored by Wauneta Hackleman and Kay Kinnaman.

General Info: No fee required. Poems may be any form and on any theme 32 lines or less. Write to the above address for complete contest rules and manuscript format instructions. You will also receive information about the many other contests sponsored annually by NFSPS. Contest entries must be mailed to: Amy and Sam Zook, 3520 St. Road 56, Mechanicsburg, OH 43044.

Prizes: Winners will receive $25 for first place; $15 for second; and $10 for third place. Selected poems may be printed in NFSPS publication, *Strophes*.

Sponsor's Remarks: "NFSPS is a non-profit organization, exclusively educational and literary. Its purpose is to recognize the importance of poetry with respect to national cultural heritage. It is dedicated solely to the furtherance of poetry on the national level and serves to unite poets in the bonds of fellowship and understanding."

† * OHIO GENEALOGICAL SOCIETY ESSAY CONTEST, sponsored by Ohio Genealogical Society, P.O. Box 2625, Mansfield, OH 44906.

General Info: Open to Ohio sophomores, juniors and seniors in public, private and parochial schools. If residing out-of-state, entrant must be a child or grandchild of OGS member. Essays are 1,500 to 1,750 words about great-grandparents or their ancestors. Proof must be submitted with entry showing descent from ancestor. Send request and SASE for more information and entry form.

Prizes: Prizes are awarded at chapter, district and state level. District winners receive one year membership to OGS. State winner receives computer, disk drive and printer. Winners also have their essay published in the *OGS Report*, a quarterly publication.

Sponsor's Remarks: "This contest promotes genealogy and encourages students to become interested in their heritage. This is the third year (1988) that the contest has been in existence."

PAUL A. WITTY OUTSTANDING LITERATURE AWARD, Cleo Bell Heiple, Chairman, 1615 2nd Ave., N., Upland, CA 91786. Sponsored by Special Interest Group, International Reading Association, Reading for Gifted and Creative Students.

General Info: Entries from elementary, junior high and high school judged separately. Two categories: prose and poetry. Elementary prose limited to 1,000 words. Entries from secondary students must be typed and may exceed 1,000 words if necessary. Set of 5 poems required. Entries judged on creativity, originality and beauty of expression. Entry blanks and more information sent to teachers on receipt of SASE.

Prizes: National awards, $25 and plaque, as deserved.

Sponsor's Remarks: "Begun in 1979 to honor Dr. Paul Witty. Between 500 and 1,000 entries are received yearly. Our goal is to encourage gifted writers by recognizing and rewarding their achievements. In past, we have given 1, 2, 4, and 5 awards and two years have found no award-worthy entries. In my correspondence with winners, I learn that most of them write continuously and go to their folio to select entries for the contest."

$ POETRY CHAPBOOK CONTEST, Trouvere Company, Rt. 2, Box 290, Eclectic, AL 36024. Annual contest for collections of poems.

General Info: Submit a collection of poetry of 32 pages, one poem per page. No poem should be longer than 40 lines. Your name and address should appear on each page for identification. Entry fee: $5. Deadline for each year: August 30.

Prizes: Grand prize, publication of the winning collection, in chapbook form, of which 100 will be printed and sent to the winner to distribute as he/she wishes. Second place, publication of the collection, in chapbook form, in which 50 will be printed and sent to the winner. Third place, same as above with 25 to be printed. Fourth place, publication of 3 selected poems from the collection in the Chapbook Contest Anthology, plus 2 copies of the anthology. Fifth through tenth place, same as for fourth except only 2 poems selected and 1 copy. Eleventh through twentieth, certificate of honorable mention with the best poem from their collection printed on it. Send SASE for complete rules.

Sponsor's Remarks: "The winners will be based on originality, quality and expressed theme. *Do not* write theme on any part of entry. We want to feel the theme come alive from the poems. Any entry that does not follow these rules will be disqualified and entry returned (if SASE is provided) or destroyed if no SASE is provided. *Sufficient* postage must be used on entries or on SASE for return of entry. The winners of 1st–20th place will not have their entry returned."

$ POETRY PRESS CONTEST, P.O. Box 739, Pittsburg, TX 75686.

General Info: Currently two categories: Rhyme and Non-Rhyme. Entrants may enter as many poems as they wish. However, the same poem cannot be entered into more than one category. Entry fee is $3 per poem or four poems for $10. Poems may not be longer than 16 lines. No line may contain more than 60 characters, including spaces. Your name and address *must* appear at the top of each entry. Type if at all possible. All entries will be destroyed 30 days after contest ends. *Retain copies of all entries.* Author retains all rights. All poems must be titled and previously unpublished. Send SASE for complete rules, current categories and deadlines.

Prizes: Prize money will be awarded to the top 3 poems in each category: $50, $25, and $10. Places 4th–25th in each category will receive honorable mention and be awared certificates of achievement. The top 100 poems in each category will be published in a category chapbook.

Sponsor's Remarks: "We attempted one Under 18 Poetry Contest. There was little response."

Subscription Rates: Copies of chapbooks may be ordered at time of entry, $5 each.

* PUBLISH-A-BOOK CONTEST, Raintree Publishers, Inc., 310 West Wisconsin Ave., Milwaukee, WI 53203. Yearly contest for grades 4, 5, or 6. Various themes.

General Info: No purchase necessary to enter. Interested students should have teacher or librarian send for contest flyer which gives current theme and deadlines. Only students currently in grades 4, 5, or 6 may enter. Stories must relate to theme. (*Example:* 1985 theme was Heritage; 1987 was Family.) Stories must be typed (by student or someone else) and be between 700 and 800 words long. Winners are selected in April. All entries become the property of the publisher.

Prizes: First place winning entry will be published in illustrated, hardcover book form and become part of the current series bearing the contest theme. Winner also receives $500 and 10 free copies of the published book. The teacher or librarian cited on the entry will receive 20 free books from the Raintree catalog. Approximate total value of first prize is $815. Each second place winner receives $25 with each sponsoring teacher or librarian receiving 10 free books from the Raintree catalog. Appriximate total value of all second prizes is $2,600. There are 20 second place winners.

Sponsor's Remarks: "Teachers and librarians may sponsor as many children as they wish for the Publish-A-Book contest."

†*$ QUILL AND SCROLL NATIONAL WRITING/PHOTOGRAPHY CONTEST, *Quill and Scroll,* School of Journalism, University of Iowa, Iowa City, IA 52242. Contest open to grades 9 to 12.

General Info: Competition open to all high school students—*Quill and Scroll* membership is not required. Each school may submit two entries in each of 10 categories: editorial, editorial cartoon, investigative reporting (individual and team), news story, feature story, sports story, advertisement, and photography (news feature and sports). Entry fee of $1 per entry must accompany each entry. Contest rules are sent, in late December, to all schools on mailing list. Guidelines and entry form also appear in the Dec/Jan issue of *Quill & Scroll* magazine. If your school does not receive information about this contest, send request for information and materials will be sent to the journalism advisor, principal, or counselors at your school. See contest guidelines sheet for format and detailed information for each category. NOTE: Senior national winners are automatically eligible for the Edward J. Nell Memorial Scholarship in Journalism.

Prizes: National winners will be notified by mail through their advisors and receive the Gold Key Award, and be listed in April/May issue of *Quill & Scroll.* Senior winners with intent to major in journalism at a college or university that offers a major in journalism are eligible for $500 scholarship.

Sponsor's Remarks: "Currently enrolled high school students are invited to enter the National Writing/Photo Contest. Awards are made in each of the ten divisions."

* $ RHYME TIME, P.O. Box 1870, Hayden, ID 83835. Various contests for writers of all ages.

General Info: Contests include short story, essay and assigned-title poetry. Also contest for previously-published poems. Entry fee is $1. No limit on number of entries you may submit. Other contests held for: quatrain, published article, essay, published short story and long poems. Some contests open to subscribers only. Entries are not returned. Send SASE for complete information on contests and themes. Sample copy is free for a #10 SASE with two first-class stamps.

Prizes: Among the prizes awarded: cash, subscriptions, publication for certain categories.

Sponsor's Remarks: "*Rhyme Time Poetry Newsletter* is a bimonthly publishing quality poetry, preferably rhymed, and fewer than 16 lines. We aim to encourage beginning poets, as well as those who are published professionals."

* SCHOLASTIC AWARDS, 730 Broadway, New York, NY 10003. Annually sponsored programs for writing, art and photography for students in grades 7–12.

General Info: Scholastic Writing Awards include classifications covering fiction, non-fiction, poetry, and drama. Scholastic Art Awards cover the fields of painting, drawing, printmaking, design, sculpture, and crafts. Scholastic Photography Awards have divisions for both black and white, and color. Complete information appears in individual rule books for *each* of the divisions, available between Oct. 1 and Jan. 1. When requesting rule books, please send postcard and specify book needed (writing, art, or photography) to above address.

Prizes: Writing Awards include cash prizes and certificates of merit. Smith-Corona also offers honor awards of portable typewriters. In addition, scholarship awards are offered by Smith-Corona, National Broadcasting Co., M.R. Robinson Fund and the Tisch School of the

Arts, NYU. Art Awards include recognition through sponsored regional exhibitions. Finalist entires, selected by regional judges, are forwarded to Scholastic for national judging. (A preliminary jury screens entries from unsponsored areas.) Regional honors include gold achievement keys and certificates of merit. National awards are gold medal plaques, scholarships, cash awards, and the honor of representation in the National High School Art Exhibition. Photography Awards are nationally co-sponsored by Eastman Kodak Co., and offer up to 250 cash awards amounting to $9,500, five scholarship grants, a $1,000 tuition scholarship offered by the Tisch School of the Arts, NYU, 15 Honorable Mention Portfolios at $100 each, and medallions of excellence selected from regional nominees. Recognition is given in the Scholastic/Kodak National Photography Exhibition. Further recognition is given through a traveling exhibit, prepared by Kodak, which tours U.S. schools, libraries, hospitals, etc.

Sponsor's Remarks: "For 62 years, the Scholastic Awards program has recognized creative achievement in Grades 7–12 in schools across the United States, Canada, and U.S. schools abroad. An estimated 250,000 entries are submitted annually in the three divisions."

* SEVENTEEN MAGAZINE/DELL FICTION CONTEST, 850 Third Avenue, New York, NY 10022. All new contest started in 1985.

General Info: Stories should be between 1,500 and 3,000 words (six to twelve pages) in length. Use standard format. Include your full name, address, and date of birth in the top right-hand corner of first page. Your last name should appear alongside the page number in the top right-hand corner of subsequent pages. You may submit as many stories as you like, but be sure to include your name, address, and birth date with each entry. Keep a copy of your story; it cannot be acknowledged or returned. Contest open to young people who are at least 13 and under 20 on January 31 of contest year. (See October issue for full details or write editor for current information.) Only original fiction that has never been published in any form, other than school publications, may be submitted. The author's signature on his or her submission will constitute acceptance of these contest rules. Be sure to follow current rules and deadline.

Prizes: Winners will receive $2,000 for first place, $1,200 for second place, $700 for third place. In addition, the work of both winners and non-winners may be considered for publication both in *Seventeen* and in future Dell Publishing Company publications.

Sponsor's Remarks: "*Seventeen* has a distinguished reputation for discovering and encouraging gifted young writers. Among the writers who were winners in previous *Seventeen* annual Fiction Contests are Perri Klass, the recipient of two O. Henry awards and "Hers" columnist for the *New York Times*; the novelist Meg Wolitzer (*Sleepwalking*, Random House); and Lorrie Moore, the author of *Self-Help* (Knopf), a critically acclaimed collection of short stories.

The first prize in *Seventeen*'s 1984 Fiction Contest was awarded to Paul Leslie—a student of Lorrie Moore at the University of Wisconsin/Madison."

Subscription Rates: Available on newsstands and by subscription.

† * **SHOE TREE CONTESTS FOR YOUNG WRITERS**, sponsored by the National Association for Young Writers, P.O. Box 228, Sandusky, MI 48471. * Writing contests for students ages 6 to 14.

General Info: Each issue sponsors a different competition in one of three categories: fiction, non-fiction, and poetry. The contests are open to all children within age range and in first grade through eighth at time of entry. All work must be original and cannot have been previously published. A statement of authenticity signed by the student and by a parent, teacher, or guardian must accompany the entry. Students may submit no more than one entry for each category. Foreign language entries welcomed if accompanied by a translation. Stories may be illustrated. Student's name, address, age, the names of his or her school and teacher must accompany the entry. Submissions should be neatly written or typed. All entries become the property of the National Association for Young Writers. Entries must be postmarked no later than January 1st (fiction); April 1st (poetry); and June 1st (non-fiction). Send SASE for complete rules.

Prizes: First prize in each of the categories is $25. Second prize in each category is a $10. The winning entries, and those given honorable mention, will be published in *Shoe Tree*.

Sponsor's Remarks: "We look for freshness and originality in the work of our prize winners. Formula stories and obvious "classroom" assignments are discouraged. Prize winners will be selected by *Shoe Tree*'s editorial staff."

Subscription Rates: Send SASE to above address for current subscription rates for *Shoe Tree* and NAYW membership information.
*Editor's note: All entries should be sent to *Shoe Tree*'s editorial office at 215 Valle del Sol, Santa, Fe, NM 87501.

* $ TAWC SPRING WRITING CONTEST, 215 Ellington St., Caro, MI 48723. Sponsored by the Thumb Area Writer's Club for amateur writers in Michigan.

General Info: You must be an amateur writer residing in the State of Michigan. For this contest, amateur is defined as (1) one who is not currently employed as a writer in the category that he/she enters; (2) one who has not sold a book or published more than 3 articles, poems, or short stories in a paying market in the category that is entered. Each entrant may submit work in any or each of three categories: short stories (1,500 words maximum), non-fiction (1,000 words maximum), poetry (32 lines maximum). You may submit up to three manuscripts in any category. Cost is $2 per each manuscript entered. Entries must be typed and follow standard format. Complete rules and current deadlines available for SASE.

Prizes: All entry fee monies will be used as cash awards and certificates. The number of entries will determine the amount of the awards. (Prizes for each of the last three years were: $15 for first place, $10 for second, $5 for third, plus several honorable mentions.) Winning entries may be published in TAWC newsletter, *Thumbprints.*

Sponsor's Remarks: "In the past, several of our place winners and honorable mention winners have been teens."

* TEENAGE FICTION CONTEST, *Teenage Magazine,* 217 Jackson St., Box 948, Lowell, MA 01853. Annual contest for writers 21 or younger.

General Info: Submissions should be received at editorial offices by February 1 for inclusion in July/August issue. Must be 21 years of age or younger. Read *Teenage* or send SASE for complete contest details and current deadlines.

Prizes: The 1985 prize was $350 plus publication of the winning entry in *TeenAge*.

Sponsor's Remarks: "We prefer short stories of 10 to 15 pages on virtually any topic. No overly sentimental, 'mushy', or juvenile romances please."

† * **TIME EDUCATION PROGRAM STUDENT WRITING CONTEST**, 10 North Main St., Yardley, PA 19067. Annual writing contest for high school students sponsored by *Time* Education Program.

General Info: High schools in the U.S. and Canada are eligible, but each student must be sponsored by a teacher. Students must enter either a 500–750 word expository composition or a piece of original art. Categories correspond to sections of *Time* magazine. Categories for writing: World, Nation, Ethics, Economy and Business. Categories for art: political cartoon, cover design, charts and maps. Deadline for 1988 is March 1. Send SASE for more information, entry blanks and future deadlines.

Prizes: College scholarships will be awarded to annual winners.

Sponsor's Remarks: "This (1988) will be the eighth annual writing contest sponsored by T.E.P. *Timelines*, a publication of the Time Education Program."

Subscription Rates: *Time* is available at newsstands and stores and by subscription.

† $ **TRI-STATE FAIR WRITING CONTESTS**, Tri State Fair, Literary Department, P.O. Box 31087, Amarillo, TX 79120. Five contest categories.

General Info: One entry fee will cover all five categories in each class. Only one entry may be submitted in each category. The same manuscript cannot be entered in more than one category. Entries must be typed. Keep your original and send a copy. Non-winning entries will be destroyed after the fair. Entry fee are: $1 for poetry, single spaced; $2 for prose, double spaced. Categories for poetry include: sonnet, nature poem, humor or light verse, narrative, portrait of a person. Prose categories are: essay, short-short story, nostalgia, how-to article, humor.

Prizes: From Tri State Fair: First place in each category, a rosette; second and third will receive ribbons. Each will receive a certificate. Other cash awards offered by various sponsoring groups. Send SASE for complete details.

Sponsor's Remarks: "This (1987) is the first contest sponsored by the Tri State Fair. We are not sure it will be held again. Write for current information."

† * VOICE OF DEMOCRACY BROADCAST SCRIPTWRITING SCHOLARSHIP PROGRAM, VFW Building, Broadway at 34th St., Kansas City, MO 64111. Annual contest sponsored by Veterans of Foreign Wars and its Ladies Auxiliary.

General Info: Open to 10th, 11th, and 12th grade students in public, parochial and private schools in the United States and overseas. Former National and/or 1st Place State winners are not eligible to compete again. U.S. citizenship is required. Scripts must not be less than three minutes nor longer than five minutes. Students may record their scripts on either cassette or reel-to-reel equipment. The script, as read by the student, should be the only sound on the tape and care should be exercised to make sure that there are no background noises or other distractions to interfere with the voice quality of the participant. There can only be one first place winner from each school and only that winner can advance in the competition. All school entries must be accepted up to November 15th except where prior arrangements have been made with the sponsoring Post and Auxiliary. Consult your school principal or assigned teacher for more information or send for program school kit with complete information and guidelines.

Prizes: First place award of $14,000 has been designated the T.C. Selman Memorial Scholarship. Total scholarships awarded: $33,500.

Sponsor's Remarks: "The Voice of Democracy Scholarship Program is the only scholarship program conducted by our organization. It is a national broadcast scriptwriting program designed to give students the opportunity to speak up for freedom and democracy."

* WRITE A PLAY, Young Playwrights Festival, The Foundation of The Dramatists Guild, 234 West 44th St., New York, NY 10036. Annual playwriting contest open to writers under the age of 19. Sponsored by the Guild with support from a number of corporations, foundations and individuals.

General Info: Scripts must be original and entirely written by one or more people who are under the age of 19 on July 1 of contest year. Scripts must be typed and securely fastened; no loose pages. Scripts must be submitted by the author(s), *not* by a teacher or parent. Submit one copy of your play and keep the original at home. Scripts will not be returned. More than one play may be submitted. Screenplays and musicals are not eligible, nor are adaptations of other author's work. On the title page, type name, date of birth, home address and phone number. Entries must be submitted no later than October 1 of contest year. Receipt of plays will be acknowledged. Participants will receive written evaluations of their work within a year of submission. Write to above address for brochure about the Young Playwrights Festival, complete contest information and tips for writing a play. Or call the Guide at (212) 575-7796.

Prizes: Selected plays will receive fully professional productions in New York City. Authors will be given one year's membership in The Dramatists Guild, America's organization for professional playwrights, and an opportunity to attend and contribute to rehearsals. Authors will also receive a royalty.

Sponsor's Remarks: "The Evaluation Program, through which each entrant receives a written evaluation of his or her work, is also supported by a grant."

* $ WRITE TO FAME, P.O. Box 248, Youngtown, AZ 85363-0248. Monthly contests in newsletter of same name sponsored by Keith Publications especially for writers ages 8 to 20.

General Info: Write for list of monthly themes. Monthly challenge open to subscribers only. Entry fees vary from 25¢ to 50¢. Some contests require no entry fee.

Prizes: Prizes vary, but include publication of winning entry and ribbon.

Sponsor's Remarks: "We are for writers ages 8 to 20, parents who understand what writing means to a child with a creative imagination, and for teachers who believe creative writing now will lead to writers in the future. My motto is 'Dream of your tomorrows and write your yesterdays today.' I encourage all young writers to write, but to succeed . . . you must submit!"

Subscription Rates: One year (12 issues) $12. Sample copy $1 plus #10 SASE.

* WRITERS OF THE FUTURE CONTEST, 2210 Wilshire Blvd., Suite 343, Santa Monica, CA 90403. Sponsored by L. Ron Hubbard.

General Info: This contest is for new or amateur writers only. All entries must be original works of science fiction or fantasy. Entries must be either short story length (under 10,000 words) or novelette length (under 17,000 words). Open only to those who have not professionally published a novel or novella or more than three short stories or one novelette. There are quarterly contests sponsored on a continuing basis. A Grand Prize winner will be selected from the quarterly winners. Write to the above address for complete rules and quarterly submission dates.

Prizes: There are three cash prizes for each quarterly contest: first $1,000; second $750; third $500. First place winners also receive a special "L. Ron Hubbard Award" trophy. Winning entries may also be printed in an anthology.

†*$ YOUNG WRITER'S CONTEST, P.O. Box 6092, McLean, VA 22106, (703) 893–6097. Conducted by Young Writer's Contest Foundation for students in grades 1 through 8. Major funder: Ronald McDonald Children's Charities.

General Info: For students in grades 1–8. Categories include short stories and poetry.

Prizes: Winners are published in *Rainbow Collection: Stories and Poetry by Young People*. Approximately 100 winners each year.

Sponsor's Remarks: "Our aim is to improve the basic communications skills of young people in the United States and to provide a different audience for writing efforts in the classroom. We have received close to 20,000 entries as of the end of our third year (1986–87). The anthology is distributed to school systems, children's hospitals, Ronald McDonald houses, retirement homes, Reading Is Fundamental, etc., where it is hoped that it will serve as inspiration to young people in addition to being of value as a sharing experience."

CHAPTER NINE

Answers to Questions Young Writers Ask Most

Why should I include a SASE?

SASE is the abbreviation for self-addressed stamped envelope. All editors and most contests insist that writers include a SASE with their manuscript. The editor will use it to send you an answer, or to return your manuscript if it is rejected. To prepare a SASE, write *your* name and address on the front of an envelope as if you were mailing it to yourself. Put the same amount of postage on your SASE that you put on your mailing envelope. (*Example:* If it costs you 56¢ to mail your manuscript, you must also put 56¢ postage on your SASE.) Put your SASE inside the mailing envelope with your manuscript.

I sent a self-addressed stamped envelope with my manuscript but I never received a reply. What should I do?

It often takes an editor 4–8 weeks to respond. If you have waited this long, send a polite letter to the editor asking if he received your manuscript and if he has made a decision. Be sure to include another self-addressed stamped envelope or self-addressed stamped postcard. Some markets receive so much mail that they cannot respond to it all. Check the market listings. If a market says, "Does not respond" or "Does not return submissions," you do not have to enclose a self-addressed stamped envelope. However, if you want to make sure an editor or contest has received your manuscript, enclose a postage-paid *postcard* addressed to you. On the note side write the title of your manuscript, the date you mailed it, and your name and address. Draw a line for the editor to mark the date it was received. (See figure 6, page 55.)

If you still receive no answer from a market that normally responds and returns manuscripts, write again asking the editor to return your manuscript. After another 3 weeks pass with no response, write or type a new copy (from the carbon or photocopy you kept) and send it to another market.

Most editors try to be as prompt as possible.

Can I send a manuscript to a publication that is not listed in *Market Guide for Young Writers*?

For various reasons, not all publications that consider material written by young people are listed in this Guide. Some editors have asked not to be listed because they prefer that only their readers submit material. If you have read a notice in a publication asking for submissions, you are considered a reader and may send them your submission whether or not they are listed in this Guide. Be careful to follow their guidelines.

There may be other publications we were not aware of or were too new at the time this edition was printed that may also consider your manuscripts. *(If you discover a market not listed in this edition, please send us their name and address so we may contact them to ask if they would like to be included in future editions.)*

Can I send the same manuscript to more than one magazine at the same time?

Sending the same manuscript to more than one market at the same time is called "simultaneous submission." It is not recommended for either adult or young writers. However, you may send different manuscripts to separate publications at the same time. Be sure to keep a record of which manuscript you sent to which market.

Most contests want only new material that has not been submitted to another contest or market before.

Why does a listing say "send holiday or seasonal material 6 months in advance"?

It takes the entire publication staff several months to collect, edit, and print a single issue. Therefore, they must consider material several months in advance of the issue's scheduled appearance. Often editors are reading Christmas stories in July and surfing stories in December. This is called the "lead time." Different publications have different lead times. Generally, a magazine's lead time is much longer than the lead time for a newspaper.

What is an International Reply Coupon?

United States postage cannot be used by publications in other countries, including Canada, to mail a letter or your manuscript back to you. If you wish to submit to a foreign market, ask a postal clerk for an International Reply Coupon to enclose with your self-addressed envelope instead of a regular postage stamp. The editor will turn in your International Reply Coupon (IRC) for proper postage.

Can my friend and I send in a story we wrote together?

Certainly. Be sure to list both your names on the manuscript.

Why doesn't my favorite magazine publish more poems by young people?

A publication is limited to how much material they can print in each issue. This is usually determined by the amount of advertising used or, in the case of publications which carry no advertising, a predetermined amount of pages. You might try writing to the editor and tell him or her that you would like to see more poems or short stories or whatever, included. It might help.

Can I write about my favorite cartoon character?

Generally speaking, young people may write about their favorite cartoon characters or other favorite fictional characters. An editor will know if a character is protected by copyright and will obtain permission if needed to publish your manuscript. However, editors prefer to read about characters you have created yourself.

My story won first place in a writing contest. Can I send it to a magazine to be printed too?

Some contests retain the copyright to entries and some do not. It should state in the rules whether you may submit your manuscript elsewhere. If the rules are not clear, write the sponsor requesting an answer. Be sure to include your name and address, the contest you entered, the title of your piece, and what awards you have won.

Do I have to subscribe to a magazine before I can send them a manuscript?

It depends. Some magazines want material only from their current readers. Two of these are *Odyssey* and *Touch*. Readers will find submission guidelines in current issues. If you don't have the magazines delivered to your home but read it in your school, library, or church, you are still considered a reader and may submit material. However, for most magazines and newspapers you do not need to subscribe before you submit material.

I don't own a typewriter. What can I do?

Some editors will accept handwritten manuscripts if they are neat and easy to read. Most markets for teens, however, require manuscripts to be typed. Try borrowing or renting a typewriter, or find someone who will type it for you. Many schools and libraries have typewriters you can use.

My story is 1,927 words long but the magazine I want to send it to only accepts stories 800 words long. Should I send it anyway?

You have three choices: (1) Cut, revise, and polish your story until you get it down to the 800 word limit, or close to it. A little over, say 50 words, is usually acceptable. Stories may always be under the word limit. (2) Look for a different publication that accepts longer stories. (3) Send it as is and take your chances. The first two suggestions are the best.

When the magazine published my story, they changed some of the words and left some parts out. I liked it better my way. Why did they do that?

There are several reasons an editor may change your story. It may have been too long to fit the available space, or he may have felt a different word or phrase made your message clearer for his readers. Writers do not always agree with the changes editors make. However, it is the editor's responsibilty to edit material if he feels it is necessary. Thankfully, most editors try not to change a writer's material. But all writers occasionally have material changed by an editor, even very famous writers.

A story I sent to a magazine was rejected. But the next issue had a story in it almost like mine. I think they stole my idea. What can I do?

First, because of a magazine's lead time (see question 5) it is very unlikely that someone stole your story. Second, many writers have the same idea for a story, though they do not write the story in the same way. Your story was probably rejected because the editor had already bought the one you had just read. Try sending your story to a different market. Ideas, by the way, are not protected by copyright.

I'm afraid someone will steal my story and publish it if I send it to an editor. Is there some way to keep people from stealing it?

It is very unlikely that anyone will steal your story, especially if it is unpublished. When a story is stolen it is called "plagiarism." Usually it is a so-called writer who steals someone else's published story and calls it his own. They are usually found out and could be taken to court.

I've never even heard of some of the magazines listed in your book. Where can I find them?

Many of the publications listed are available by subscription only, although some are available at libraries and stores. If you are interested in submitting to a magazine you have never read, it's best to send for a sample copy. Most editors will send a writer a sample copy for free, or if you include a self-addressed stamped envelope with your request, or for a small fee. Check the market listing for that information.

Do I have to submit to magazines only for kids, or can I send material to the ones my parents read, too?

There are a number of magazines for adults that publish material from young people. Some like *Grit* are listed in this Guide. For other publications, you might be able to express your opinion on a certain topic and address it to: Letter to the Editor.

Why should I bother sending my material to a publication that doesn't pay for it?

As a young writer, you should be more interested in getting your work published rather than making a lot of money for it. In fact, very few writers of any age get rich writing for magazines alone. You will gain valuable experience with every sale you make to a publication whether you are paid or not. Of course, you can choose not to send material to a publication that does not pay young writers. It is entirely up to you.

Why do some magazines pay a lot for manuscripts, some just a little, and some not at all?

How much a publication pays for a manuscript varies greatly according to the publication's operating budget and editorial policy. In general, the markets listed in this Guide, which normally pay for material, pay the same rates to young people as they do to adults.

On some guidelines I've read "pays on acceptance" and on others "pays on publication." What's the difference?

A publication which "pays on acceptance" will send you your check soon after your manuscript is accepted, without waiting for it to be actually published. Markets that "pay on publication" wait until they have actually printed your manuscript in an issue before sending you a check. Waiting for a "pays on publication" market to pay you is sometimes very frustrating. It may take up to a year or longer before your manuscript is published.

Do I have to cash the check I got from a magazine? I want to frame it.

By all means, cash it. Consider framing your printed piece instead. You might also consider framing a photocopy of the check or single dollar bill along with your check stub to signify your first "for pay" sale.

An article I submitted was rejected because they had printed a similar piece a few months before. How can I know what subjects have been covered without reading every back issue of every magazine I'd like to submit to?

This happens most with information or how-to articles. Have your school or public librarian show you how to use two reference collections called *Readers Guide to Periodic Literature* and the *Children's Magazine Guide*. Both list by subject, title, and author articles published in many publications. However, don't worry too much if your subject has been covered recently if you've written an essay or opinion piece. Editors often repeat certain subjects if the writer presents a different or interesting viewpoint.

What is a "theme list?"

Some magazines plan monthly issues around a certain topic or theme, such as medicine, sports heroes, dating, etc. Most market listings will specify if a publication follows a theme list. You may write for a list of upcoming themes. The deadline dates for submitting material will be included to help you meet their lead time.

I'm confused. Do I send my original manuscript and keep the copy or do I send the copy and keep my original?

Generally, you would send your original manuscript and keep the copy. However, some contests differ. Check a list of the current rules carefully and send what they specify.

What should I do with material that is rejected?

First of all, try hard not to take it personally. There are many reasons a manuscript may be rejected and some have nothing to do with how well, or how poorly, it is written. Reread your work and see if you can improve it. If you like it the way it is, look for another market. Even famous writers have material rejected. Some manuscripts are not bought until the fifth or even the thirtieth submission. The key is to keep trying.

What does "copyright" mean?

For writers "copy" means their written work. "Right" refers to the person who has the authority to sell a certain piece of written, drawn or photographed work. When you write something, you automatically become the copyright owner by law. If an editor agrees to publish your manuscript, he will "buy the rights" to it. There are various rights you may grant an editor or contest. Generally, magazines buy "one-time rights" which gives them permission to print your manuscript one time. Then the rights are returned to you and you may offer the same manuscript to another editor for "second" or "reprint" rights. A number of publications buy "all rights" which means that once you agree the publication can print your manuscript, it becomes their property and is no longer yours. You may not send it to another market. Most articles published in newspapers enter what is known as "public domain" and may be reprinted, or the information used, by anyone, though credit is usually given to the original source. Sometimes you will see a copyright notice on a newspaper article which is of special importance or on a subject of great interest. The copyright notice protects that particular newpaper article from being reprinted without written permission.

Copyrights can be very confusing. For more information about current copyright laws and a free list of other government brochures write to: United States Copyright Office, Library of Congress, Washington, DC 20599.

My aunt told me about a place in Washington, D.C., where I can get a patent so no one will be able to publish my story unless I say so. Do you know the address?

What you need is information about "copyrights" which, by law, protect a writer's work from being used without permission. See the answer to the previous question for the correct address of the United States Copyright Office.

What is a model release form?

Occasionally a publication will ask the writer to provide a statement signed by the person granting an interview or photograph to prove that he or she agreed to being interviewed and/or photographed. One such publication that asks for a model release form is *Grit*. You can make your own model release form using a clean sheet of paper containing your name, address, phone number, and the name, address, phone number of the person being interviewed or photographed. Have that person write a sentence or two which shows he or she understands that the information or photograph may be published, then sign his or her name and the date. Most people don't mind providing this information. If you are writing something about someone eighteen or younger, or will be taking their picture, have a parent or guardian also sign the model release form. You do not need to provide this form unless the publication's guidelines specifically request it.

Should I include a letter with my manuscript when I mail it?

If there is special information that you would like to tell the editor which is not included in your manuscript, you may send a short, one page letter. This is called a "cover letter." Most times this is not necessary.

What is a query letter?

Writers send a "query letter" to editors when they want to know in advance whether the editor would be interested in receiving a manuscript about a certain topic. Editors prefer that young writers send a complete manuscript, though older teens attempting to publish in adult publications may send query letters outlining their proposed article. Check the reference list included in this Guide for additional information on this subject.

Someday, if you've sold several manuscripts to the same editor, you may be surprised to receive a query letter yourself from that editor asking you to write on a certain subject. The editor will feel confident doing this because he is already familiar with your previous work and knows that you can be depended upon to complete a writing project. Of course, it will be up to you whether or not you accept the assignment.

Common Editing Marks

Use these symbols to make simple corrections on a manuscript. Write the correct information directly above the mistake if it is only one or two words. To add a complete sentence or paragraph, write "Insert Copy A." At the bottom, or on another sheet, write Copy A with the correct information. If you must insert information in more than one place, label them "Copy B, Copy C, etc." Delete words by drawing the "delete" symbol through the word. For more than one word, draw a line through everything that is to be deleted, and place the delete symbol in the middle.

#	Insert space	ℋ	Start new paragraph
⊙	Add period	ℒ	Delete word or phrase
A̸	Use lower case	*Stet*	Disregard the correction
a̲̲	Use upper case	∧	Insert
⊂	Close up space	∨	Insert
Sam⫽ple	Transpose		

Resources

Books for Beginning Writers

Books for You to Make, Susan Purdy. Lippincott, 1973.

How to Read and Write Poetry, Anna Cosman. Franklin Watts, 1979.

In Your Own Words, Sylvia Cassedy. Doubleday, 1979.

Let's Write Short Stories, Arnold Cheyney. Seamon, 1973.

Poetry Is, Ted Hughes. Doubleday, 1970.

Putting on a Play: A Guide to Writing and Producing Neighborhood Drama, Susan and Stephen Judy. Scribners, 1982.

Where Do You Get Your Ideas? Sandy Asher, Walker, 1987.

Write Your Own Story, Vivian Dubrovin. Franklin Watts, 1984.

Writing for Kids, Carol Lea Benjamin. Harper and Row, 1985.

Your Career as a Writer, Mary Lewis Hanson. Arco, 1979.

Books for Advanced Pre-Teens and Teens

How I Came to Be a Writer, Phyllis Naylor. Atheneum, 1978.

How to Write and Sell Your Personal Experiences, Lois Duncan. Writer's Digest Books, 1984.

Make Every Word Count, Gary Provost. Writer's Digest Books, 1980.

Writing for Children and Teenagers, Lee Wyndham. Writer's Digest Books, 1972.

Writing from the Inside Out, Charlotte Edwards. Writer's Digest Books, 1984.

Writing the Natural Way, Gabriele Lusser Rico. J.P. Tarcher, 1983.

Books for Teachers and Parents

Any Child Can Write: How to Improve Your Child's Writing Skills from Preschool Through High School, Harvey S. Weiner, Ph.D. McGraw-Hill, 1978.

Can't Anybody Here Write? Stephen K. Smuin. Mushroom Enterprises, 1981.

Creative Writing, A Handbook for Teaching Young People, Kathyleen C. Phillips and Barbara Steiner. Libraries Unlimited, 1985.

How to Capture Live Authors and Bring Them to Your Schools, David Melton. Landmark Editions, 1986.

Written & Illustrated by . . . , David Melton. Landmark Editions, 1985.

Magazines for Writers

Byline. Subscription Department, P.O. Box 130596, Edmond, OK 73140.

The Writer. Subscription Department, 120 Boylston Street, Boston, MA 02116.

Writer's Digest. Subscription Department, 205 W. Center Street, Marion, OH 43305.

Writing! General Learning Corporation, P.O. Box 310, Highwood, IL 60040.

Wordworks, Young Writers' Newsletter. Subscription Department, P.O. Box 216, Newburyport, MA 01950.

Organizations

National Association for Young Writers, P.O. Box 452, Belvidere, NJ 07823.

National Association of Young Authors, 3015 Woodsdale Blvd., Lincoln, NE 68502.

Words Writers Use

angle. "To angle" a piece of writing means to choose a subject of special interest to a particular publication and to write about one aspect of that subject in a style similar to what that publication usually uses. (See slant.)

article. A piece of writing based on facts rather than fiction. News, how-to, essays, opinions, profiles, etc., are all types of articles.

B & W. Black and white photos or drawings.

byline. The line printed above a newspaper or magazine article telling who wrote the piece.

caption. Written material which describes the subject matter of a photo or illustration. Also called "cutline."

chapbook. A small booklet, usually paperback, with collections of poetry, ballads, or stories.

clippings. Short items of interest cut from (clipped) a magazine or newspaper. Also a copy of a manuscript clipped from the publication in which it was published.

contract. A written agreement specifying which rights an editor is buying and what payment the writer will receive for a manuscript.

contributor's copies. Free issues of a publication which you receive instead of, or in addition to, payment.

clean-copy. A manuscript which has no errors and needs no editing.

copy. A term for the contents of a manuscript.

correspondent. A person who regularly supplies a publication with articles.

cut. To trim unnecessary parts of a manuscript to make it read better or to fit available space.

deadline. The last day a contest entry will be accepted or the date on which an editor expects to receive a manuscript that he intends to publish.

draft. What you call your piece of writing while you are creating it.

edit. To correct, cut, or otherwise alter a manuscript in the hopes of improving it.

editor. A person who edits; also a person who among other responsibilities, accepts or rejects manuscripts for publication and has the authority to edit material.

feature. A non-fiction article which usually gives extra background information about a subject.

filler. A short item of interest used in a publication to fill in leftover space before printing.

final draft. A manuscript which has been written, corrected, and prepared for submitting to a market.

freelance writer. A person who writes fiction, non-fiction, or poetry on his own, then selects markets to submit it to.

illustrations. Photographs or artwork used alone or with a manuscript which are sometimes supplied by the writer.

international reply coupon (IRC). Special coupons which writers can buy at the post office to include with a self-addressed envelope for use by markets in countries outside the U.S.

lead time. The amount of time needed by a publication to collect and prepare material for use in an upcoming issue.

manuscript. A creative written work prepared on paper.

market. Any publication or contest which considers material from writers with or without the possibility of payment.

masthead. The section in a newspaper, magazine, or other publication giving the publication's name, the owner's name, and the names of the staff members including the editor.

model release form. A paper signed by someone being interviewed or photographed giving permission to use the material or photo for a specific purpose. If the person is a minor, the paper must also be signed by a parent or guardian.

query. A one-page letter asking an editor if he would be interested in seeing a particular manuscript you have written, or would like to write.

rights. What you offer to an editor in exchange for printing your manuscripts.

rough draft. A manuscript which has been written but not checked for errors in grammar, punctuation, spelling or content. It usually needs revision and rewriting.

SASE. An envelope with postage attached and addressed to you which is included in the envelope containing your manuscript or letter when submitting to an editor or other person from whom you would like a response.

slant. To mold an idea for a manuscript to fit the particular needs of a publication, such as writing related to sports, religion, exercise, stickers, etc. (See angle.)

slush pile. What editors call the collection of submitted manuscripts which have not been specifically asked for.

solicited manuscript. Material which an editor has asked for or agreed to consider before being sent by the writer.

speculation. When an editor agrees in advance to look at your manuscript but there is no guarantee he will accept it for publication, the editor says he will look at it "on speculation;" also "on spec."

tearsheet. A sample of your printed piece which has been taken (torn) following publication from the publication in which it was printed. Can also be a photocopy of your published work.

"to market." To submit your manuscript to a publication in the hopes of having it accepted for publication.

transparencies. Developed color slides, not color prints.

unsolicited manuscripts. Material which is submitted to a publication which an editor did not specifically ask to see.

vanity publisher. A publisher who charges a writer the cost of publishing a manuscript, usually a book. Also called subsidy publisher.

word length. The maximum number of words a manuscript should contain as determined by the editor or guidelines sheet.

Index

ABOUT THE AUTHOR

Kathy Henderson is executive director of the National Association for Young Writers, and a member of the NAYW Board of Trustees. She works closely with children through young authors conferences and writers workshops, and is a frequent guest speaker in schools.

A freelance writer for the past seventeen years, she has had hundreds of articles and stories published in numerous publications, including *Child Life, Jack and Jill,* the *Detroit News Sunday Magazine* and many others.

Mrs. Henderson has also served as the Michigan Advisor for the Society of Children's Book Writers, and has her own column in *Kinderbook.* She lives on a 300 acre dairy farm in Michigan with her husband, Keith, and two teenage children.

Notes

Notes

Notes

Notes